Living L
CONVERS
ITALIAN

REVISED AND UPDATED

THE LIVING LANGUAGE™ SERIES

LIVING LANGUAGE ™ Complete Courses, Revised & Updated

*French**
*German**
Inglés/English for Spanish Speakers
*Italian**
*Japanese**
Portuguese (Brazilian)
Portuguese (Continental)
Russian
*Spanish**

*Also available on Compact Disc

LIVING LANGUAGE ™ Complete Courses

Advanced French
Advanced Spanish
Children's French
Children's Spanish
English for Chinese Speakers
English for French Speakers
English for German Speakers
English for Italian Speakers
Hebrew

LIVING LANGUAGE IN-TENSE ™ Verb Practice

French, German, Italian, Spanish

LIVING LANGUAGE PLUS®

French, German, Italian, Spanish

LIVING LANGUAGE TRAVELTALK ™

French, German, Italian, Japanese
Portuguese, Russian, Spanish

LIVING LANGUAGE ™ SPEAK UP!® Accent Elimination Courses

American Regional
Spanish
Asian, Indian, and Middle Eastern

LIVING LANGUAGE ™ FAST & EASY

Arabic
Czech
French
German
Hebrew
Hungarian
Inglés/English for Spanish Speakers
Italian
Japanese
Korean
Mandarin Chinese
Polish
Portuguese
Russian
Spanish

Living Language™

CONVERSATIONAL ITALIAN

REVISED AND UPDATED

Revised by Lorraine-Marie Gatto

Based on the original
by Genevieve A. Martin
and Mario Ciatti

Based on the method devised
by Ralph Weiman, Former Chief of
Language Section, U.S. War Department

CROWN PUBLISHERS, INC., NEW YORK

This work was previously published under the title *Conversation Manual Italian.*

Published by Crown Publishers, Inc., 201 East 50th Street, New York, New York 10022. Member of the Crown Publishing Group.

Random House, Inc. New York, Toronto, London, Sydney, Auckland.

Manufactured in the United States of America

Library of Congress Catalog Card Number: 56-9317

ISBN 0-517-59039-5

10 9 8

CONTENTS

INTRODUCTION

Living Language™ Italian makes it easy to learn how to speak, read, and write Italian. This course is a thoroughly revised and updated version of *Living Italian: The Complete Living Language Course®*. The same highly effective method of language instruction is still used, but the content has been updated to reflect modern usage, and the format has been clarified. In this course, the basic elements of the language have been carefully selected and condensed into forty short lessons. If you can study about thirty minutes a day, you can master this course and learn to speak Italian in a few weeks.

This *Living Language™ Conversational Italian* manual provides English translations and brief explanations for each lesson. The first five lessons cover pronunciation, laying the foundation for learning the vocabulary, phrases, and grammar, which are explained in the later chapters. If you already know a little Italian, you can use the book as a phrasebook and reference. In addition to the forty lessons, there is a Summary of Italian Grammar, plus verb conjugations, and a section on writing letters.

Also included in the course package is the *Living Language™ Italian Dictionary*. It contains more than 15,000 entries, with many of the definitions illustrated by phrases and idiomatic expressions. More than 1,000 of the most essential words are capitalized to make them easy to find. You can increase your vocabulary and range of expression just by browsing through the dictionary.

Practice your Italian as much as possible, even if you can't manage a trip abroad. Watching Italian movies, reading Italian magazines, eating at Italian restaurants, and talking with Italian speaking friends are enjoyable ways to help reinforce what you have learned with *Living Language™ Conversational Italian*. Now, let's begin.

The following instructions will tell you what to do. *Buona fortuna!* Good luck!

COURSE MATERIAL

1. Two 90-minute cassettes or three 60-minute compact discs.

2. *Living Language™ Conversational Italian* manual. This book is designed for use with the recorded lessons, but it may also be used alone as a reference. It contains the following sections:

Basic Italian in 40 Lessons
Summary of Italian Grammar
Verb Conjugations
Letter Writing

3. *Living Language™ Italian Dictionary.* The Italian/English-English/Italian dictionary contains more than 15,000 entries. Phrases and idiomatic expressions illustrate many of the definitions. More than 1,000 of the most essential words are capitalized.

INSTRUCTIONS

1. Look at page 1. The words in **boldface** type are the ones you will hear on the recording.
2. Now read Lesson 1 all the way through. Note the points to listen for when you play the recording. The first word you will hear is **Alfredo.**
3. Start the recording, listen carefully, and say the words aloud in the pauses provided. Go through the lesson once and don't worry if you can't pronounce everything correctly the first time around. Try it again and keep repeating the lesson until you are comfortable with it. The more often you listen and repeat, the longer you will remember the material.
4. Now go on to the next lesson. If you take a break between lessons, it's always good to review the previous lesson before starting on a new one.

5. In the manual, there are two kinds of quizzes. With matching quizzes, you must select the English translation of the Italian sentence. The other type requires you to fill in the blanks with the correct Italian word chosen from the three given directly below the sentence. If you make any mistakes, begin again and reread the section.
6. Even after you have finished the forty lessons and achieved a perfect score on the Final Quiz, keep practicing your Italian by listening to the recordings and speaking with Italian-speaking friends. For further study, try *Living Language Plus® Italian, Living Language In-Tense™ Italian Verb Practice,* and *Living Language Traveltalk™ Italian.*

Living Language™
CONVERSATIONAL
ITALIAN
REVISED AND UPDATED

LESSON 1

A. Sounds of the Italian Language

Many Italian sounds are similar to the English. Listen to and repeat the following Italian names, and notice which sounds are similar and which are different:

Alfredo	Alfred	**Luigi**	Louis
Antonio	Antonio	**Luisa**	Louise
Carlo	Charles	**Maria**	Mary
Caterina	Katherine	**Michele**	Michael
Enrico	Henry	**Paolo**	Paul
Elisabetta	Elizabeth	**Peppino**	Joe
Emmanuele	Emanuel	**Pietro**	Peter
Ferdinando	Ferdinand	**Raffaele**	Raphael
Francesco	Francis	**Raimondo**	Raymond
Giovanni	John	**Riccardo**	Richard
Giorgio	George	**Roberto**	Robert
Giulia	Julia	**Rosa**	Rose
Giuseppe	Joseph	**Vincenzo**	Vincent
Isabella	Isabel	**Violetta**	Violet

NOTE:

a. that each vowel is pronounced clearly and crisply.

b. that a single consonant is pronounced with the following vowel.

c. that some vowels bear an accent mark, which sometimes shows the accentuated syllable:

la città the city

but sometimes merely serves to distinguish words:

e and **è** is

d. When the accent is on the letter *e*, it gives a more open pronunciation:

caffè coffee

e. The apostrophe (') is used to mark elision, the omission of a vowel. For example, when the word *dove* (where) is combined with *è* (is), the *e* in *dove* is dropped: *Dov'è*? Where is?

Now listen to some geographical names:

Bari	**Napoli**
Brindisi	**Ravenna**
Genova	**Sardegna**
Legnano	**Sicilia**
Livorno	**Taranto**
Messina	**Urbino**
Milano	**Venezia**

Now the names of some countries:

Argentina	**Inghilterra**
Belgio	**Messico**
Cina	**Norvegia**
Spagna	**Giappone**
Stati Uniti	**Portogallo**
India	**Egitto**
Francia	**Venezuela**
Germania	**Russia**

B. COGNATES: WORDS SIMILAR IN ENGLISH AND ITALIAN

Now listen to and repeat the following cognates (words which are similar in English and Italian). Notice how Italian spelling and pronunciation differ from English:

azione	action	**centro**	center
agente	agent	**certo**	certain
attenzione	attention	**differente**	different
caso	case	**difficile**	difficult

esempio	example	**radio**	radio
festa	feast	**ristorante**	restaurant
chitarra	guitar	**simile**	similar
importante	important	**té**	tea
interessante	interesting	**teatro**	theater
nazione	nation	**telefono**	telehpone
necessario	necessary	**treno**	train
possibile	possible	**visita**	visit
quieto	quiet		

LESSON 2

A. The Italian Alphabet

LETTER	NAME	LETTER	NAME	LETTER	NAME
a	a	**h**	acca	**q**	qu
b	bi	**i**	i	**r**	erre
c	ci	**l**	elle	**s**	esse
d	di	**m**	emme	**t**	ti
e	e	**n**	enne	**u**	u
f	effe	**o**	o	**v**	vi
g	gi	**p**	pi	**z**	zeta

B. Pronunciation Practice with Cognates

The following groups of cognates will give you some additional practice in Italian pronunciation and spelling:

attore	actor	**generoso**	generous
animale	animal	**generale**	general
capitale	capital	**umore**	humor
centrale	central	**locale**	local
cereale	cereal	**materiale**	material
cioccolato	chocolate	**originale**	original
colore	color	**personale**	personal
dottore	doctor	**probabile**	probable
familiare	familiar	**regolare**	regular

simile	similar	**totale**	total
semplice	simple	**usuale**	usual

LESSON 3

A. VOWELS

1. *a* is like *ah,* or the *a* in *father:*

a	to, at	**lago**	lake
amico	friend	**pane**	bread
la	the (*fem.sing.*)[1]	**parlare**	to speak

2. *e* is like the *ay* in *day,* but cut off sharply (that is, not drawled):

era	was	**treno**	train
essere	to be	**tre**	three
pera	pear	**estate**	summer
padre	father	**se**	if
carne	meat		

e in the middle of a word may have two different sounds when stressed:

OPEN SOUND		CLOSED SOUND	
petto	chest	**verde**	green
terra	earth		

Some words even have different meanings according to whether the vowel has an open or closed sound:

OPEN SOUND		CLOSED SOUND	
tema	composition	**tema**	fear
venti	winds	**venti**	twenty

[1] *fem sing.* stands for *feminine singular.* In Italian, nouns are either masculine or feminine, and the words that modify them agree in gender and number (singular or pural).

3. *i* is like the *i* in *police, machine, marine,* but not drawled:

misura	measure	**oggi**	today
sì	yes	**piccolo**	small *(masc.sing.)*
amica	friend *(fem.)*	**figlio**	son

4. *o* is like the *o* in *no,* but not drawled:

no	no	**con**	with
poi	then	**otto**	eight
ora	hour	**come**	how

5. *o* in the middle of a word may have two different sounds when stressed.

OPEN SOUND		CLOSED SOUND	
sono	am, are	**forma**	form
corpo	body	**voce**	voice

6. *u* is like the *u* in *rule,* but not drawled:

uno	one *(masc.)*	**tu**	you *(familiar)*[1]
una	one *(fem.)*	**ultimo**	last

7. Notice that each vowel is clearly pronounced. Vowels are not slurred as they often are in English:

Europa	Europe	**poesia**	poem
leggere	to read	**creare**	to create
dov'è	where is	**mio**	my
io sono	I am	**paese**	country
idea	idea		

[1] Italian distinguished between familiar and formal forms of "you" both in the singular and the plural. The *tu* form is reserved for children, close friends, and relatives. Use the *Lei* form, which is more polite, for people you have just met, as well as with professionals and others you wish to show respect for.

B. DIPHTHONGS: DOUBLE VOWEL COMBINATIONS

1. *ai:*

guai troubles

2. *au:*

aula room **autunno** autumn

3. *ei:*

sei six **dei** of the

4. *eu:*

Europa Europe **neutro** neutral

5. *ai:*

Italia Italy **patria** country

6. *ie*

piede foot **tieni** (you) keep

7. *io:*

stazione staion **piove** it is raining

8. *iu:*

fiume river **piuma** feather

9. *oi:*

poi then **noi** we

10. *ua:*

quale what **quattro** four

11. *ue:*

questo this **quello** that

12. *ui:*

buio darkness **lui** him

13. *uo:*

buono good **tuo** your (*familiar*)

or in certain forms of the verb to have:

io ho I have

7. *l, m, n, p,* are equivalent to the corresponding letters in English:

libertà	liberty	**notte**	night
memoria	memory	**prova**	proof

8. *q* is used only in combination with *u* and is pronounced like the English *qu* in *quality.*

quarto quarter

9. *r* is more rolled than in English, similar to Spanish pronunciation:

regione region

10. *s* has two different sounds:
    a. hard at the beginning of a word, or when used double, or when followed by another consonant:

sale	salt	**fresco**	cool
rosso	red		

b. soft when occurring between two vowels:

causa	cause	**poesia**	poetry
esilio	exile		

11. *t, v,* are equivalent to the corresponding letters in English:

tono	tone	**vacanza**	vacation

12. *z* has two different sounds:
    a. harsh, as in the English combination *ts.* This sound generally occurs in the group *-zione.*

azione	action	**addizione**	addition
nazione	nation		

b. soft, as in the English combination *ds.* This sound occurs mostly in technical and classical words derived from Greek.

zona	zone	**zebra**	zebra

B. Special Italian Sounds

Pay special attention to the following sounds, which do not have exact English equivalents:

1. *cc* when followed by *i* or *e* is pronounced like the English *ch* in *chair:*

cacciatore	hunter	**faccia**	face

2. *ch* before *e* and *i* is pronounced like the English *k* in *key:*

chitarra	guitar	**chiodo**	nail

3. *gh* before *e* and *i* is pronounced like the English *g* in *gate:*

ghiaccio	ice	**ghetto**	ghetto

4. *gli* is a sound found only in Italian; the closest English approximation would be the combination *lli,* as in *million:*

figlia	daughter	**paglia**	straw
foglia	leaf	**giglio**	lily

5. *gn* is always pronounced as one letter, somewhat like the English *ni* in *onion,* or *ny* in *canyon:*

segno	sign	**Spagna**	Spain
montagna	mountain	**lavagna**	blackboard

6. *sc* before *e* and *i* is pronounced like the English *sh* in *shoe:*

scendere	(to) climb	**sciroppo**	syrup
scimmia	monkey	**scivolare**	(to) slip

7. *sc* before *a, o,* and *u,* is pronounced like the English *sk* in *sky:*

scuola	school	**Scozia**	Scotland
scarpa	shoe	**scoiattolo**	squirrel

C. More Italian-English Cognates

Building up an Italian vocabulary is fairly easy since a great number of words are similar in English and Italian. Some words are spelled exactly the same (though they may differ considerably in pronunciation):

ITALIAN	ENGLISH	ITALIAN	ENGLISH
antenna	antenna	**zoo**	zoo
area	area	**idea**	idea
auto	auto	**opera**	opera
radio	radio	**cinema**	cinema

There are many Italian words that you will have no difficulty in recognizing despite minor differences. Some of these differences are:

1. The Italian words add *e*.

annuale	annual	**origine**	origin
occasionale	occasional	**speciale**	special
parte	part		

2. The Italian words add *a* or *o*.

lista	list	**costo**	cost
problema	problem	**liquido**	liquid
persona	person		

3. The Italian words have *a* or *o* where the English ones have *e*.

causa	cause	**favorito**	favorite
figura	figure	**minuto**	minute
medicina	medicine	**tubo**	tube
rosa	rose	**uso**	use

D. General Spelling Equivalents

1. Italian *c (cc)* = English *k (ck):*

franco frank **parco** park
sacco sack **attacco** attack

2. Italian *f* = English *ph:*

frase phrase **telefono** telephone
fisico physical **fonico** phonic

3. Italian *s (ss)* = English *x:*

esercizio exercise **Messico** Mexico
esempio example **fisso** fix

4. Italian *st* = English *xt:*

estensione extension **estremo** extreme
esterno external

5. Italian *t* = English *th:*

autore author **teatro** theatre
simpatia sympathy **teoria** theory

6. Italian *z (zz)* = English *c:*

forza force **razza** race

7. Italian *i* = English *y:*

stile style **sistema** system
mistero mystery **ritmo** rhythm

8. Italian *o* = English *ou:*

corte court **corso** course
montagne mountain

9. Italian *-io* = English *-y:*

segretario secretary **territorio** territory

10. Italian *-zione* = English *-tion:*

nazione nation **addizione** addition

11. Italian *-o* = English *-al:*

interno internal **politico** political
eterno eternal

12. Italian *-oso* = English *-ous:*

famoso	famous	**generoso**	generous
numeroso	numerous	**religioso**	religious

LESSON 5

A. Numbers 1–10

uno	one
due	two
tre	three
quattro	four
cinque	five
sei	six
sette	seven
otto	eight
nove	nine
dieci	ten

Uno più uno fa due.	One and one are two.
Uno più due fa tre.	One and two are three.
Due più due fanno quattro.	Two and two are four.
Due più tre fanno cinque.	Two and three are five.
Tre più tre fanno sei.	Three and three are six.
Tre più quattro fanno sette.	Three and four are seven.
Quattro più quattro fanno otto.	Four and four are eight.
Cinque più quattro fanno nove.	Five and four are nine.
Cinque più cinque fanno dieci.	Five and five are ten.

B. Days of the Week[1]

lunedì	Monday
martedì	Tuesday
mercoledì	Wednesday

[1]The names of the days of the week and of the months are never capitalized.

giovedì	Thursday
venerdì	Friday
sabato	Saturday
domenica	Sunday

C. Months of the Year

gennaio	January
febbraio	February
marzo	March
aprile	April
maggio	May
giugno	June
luglio	July
agosto	August
settembre	September
ottobre	October
novembre	November
dicembre	December

D. Seasons

primavera	spring
estate	summer
autunno	autumn
inverno	winter

E. North, South, East, West

nord	north
sud	south
est	east
ovest	west

F. Morning, Noon, and Night

mattina	morning
mezzogiorno	noon
pomeriggio	afternoon
sera	evening
notte	night

G. Today, Yesterday, Tomorrow

oggi	today
ieri	yesterday
domani	tomorrow
Oggi è venerdì.	Today is Friday.
Ieri era giovedì.	Yesterday was Thursday.
Domani è sabato.	Tomorrow is Saturday.

H. Colors

rosso	red
blu	blue
verde	green
nero	black
bianco	white
giallo	yellow
marrone	brown (coffee-color)
castagno	brown (chestnut-color)
grigio	gray

QUIZ 1

Try matching these two columns:

1. *venerdì*	a. January
2. *autunno*	b. summer
3. *giovedì*	c. June
4. *primavera*	d. winter

5.	*otto*	e.	October
6.	*gennaio*	f.	white
7.	*inverno*	g.	autumn
8.	*verde*	h.	Sunday
9.	*giugno*	i.	eight
10.	*estate*	j.	spring
11.	*lunedì*	k.	west
12.	*quattro*	l.	Thursday
13.	*ottobre*	m.	four
14.	*domenica*	n.	ten
15.	*ovest*	o.	red
16.	*rosso*	p.	black
17.	*nero*	q.	green
18.	*dieci*	r.	Friday
19.	*bianco*	s.	gray
20.	*grigio*	t.	Monday

ANSWERS

1—r; 2—g; 3—l; 4—j; 5—i; 6—a; 7—d; 8—q; 9—c; 10—b; 11—t; 12—m; 13—e; 14—h; 15—k; 16—o; 17—p; 18—n; 19—f; 20—s.

LESSON 6

A. Greetings

DI MATTINA	IN THE MORNING
buon	good
giorno	morning (day)[1]
Buon giorno.	Good morning.
Signor	Mr.
Rossi.	Rossi.
Buon giorno, signor Rossi.	Good morning, Mr. Rossi.
Salve	Hello (*polite*)
Ciao	Hello/Good-bye (*familiar*)
come	how

[1] Words in parentheses are literal translations.

sta	are you
Come sta?	How are you? How do you do? (*polite*)
Come stai?	How are you? (*familiar*)
molto	very
bene	well
Molto bene.	Very well.
grazie	thank you, thanks
Molto bene, grazie.	Very well, thank you.
E Lei? [1]	And how are you? (And you?)
E tu?	And you? (*familiar*)
bene	fine
Bene grazie.	Fine, thank you.
Arrivederci.	Good-bye. (*polite*)
Ciao.	Good-bye. (*familiar*)

DI SERA	IN THE EVENING
buona	good
sera	evening
Buona sera.	Good afternoon. Good evening.
Buona sera, signora Rossi	Good afternoon, Mrs. Rossi. Good evening, Mrs. Rossi.
Buona notte.	Good night.
Buona notte, signorina Rossi.	Good night, Miss Rossi.

Note: The Italian word for "sir" or "Mr." is *signore,* but when it is used immediately preceding a name, the *e* is dropped.

Buon giorno, signor Rossi.
Buon giorno, signore.

[1] Italian has both a polite, formal form of "you" (*Lei*) and an informal, familiar form (*tu*). Use *tu* when talking to family, good friends, or children. In other situations, it's better to err on the side of politeness and use *Lei*.

B. How's the Weather?

Che tempo fa oggi?	What's the weather today?
Fa bel tempo.	It's nice (beautiful) weather.
Fa brutto tempo.	It's awful (ugly) weather.
Fa freddo.	It's cold.
Fa fresco.	It's cool.
Fa caldo.	It's hot.
Piove.	It's raining.
Nevica.	It's snowing.
C'è il sole.	It's sunny.
È nuvoloso	It's cloudy.
Tira vento.	It's windy.

QUIZ 2

1. *mattina*	a. Good afternoon, Good evening
2. *signora*	b. How are you? (*polite*)
3. *E Lei?*	c. Miss
4. *molto bene*	d. morning
5. *Buon giorno.*	e. Thank you.
6. *Buona notte.*	f. Madam or Mrs.
7. *Come sta?*	g. How are you? (*familiar*)
8. *Piove.*	h. sir or Mr.
9. *Grazie*	i. What's the weather today?
10. *Come stai?*	j. Good morning.
11. *signorina*	k. It's nice weather.
12. *Buona sera.*	l. And you?
13. *Que tempo fa oggi?*	m. very well

14. *signore* — n. It's raining.

15. *Fa bel tempo.* — o. Good night.

ANSWERS

1—d; 2—f; 3—l; 4—m; 5—j; 6—o; 7—b; 8—n; 9—e; 10—g; 11—c; 12—a; 13—i; 14—h; 15—k.

C. WORD STUDY

classe	class
considerabile	considerable
differenza	difference
elemento	element
gloria	glory
operazione	operation
madre	mother
padre	father

LESSON 7

A. WHERE IS ...?

dove	where
è	is
dov'è (dove è)	where is
Dov'è un albergo?	Where is a hotel?
buon ristorante	good restaurant
Dov'è un buon ristorante?	Where's a good restaurant?
dov'è	where is
Dov'è?	Where is it?
Dov'è il telefono?	Where's the telephone?
Dov'è il ristorante?	Where's the restaurant?
Dov'è la toletta?	Where's the bathroom?
Dov'è la stazione ferroviaria?	Where's the railroad station?
Dov'è l'ufficio postale?	Where's the post office?

B. Can You Tell Me?

può dirmi Lei	can you tell me
Può dirmi Lei dov'è un albergo?	Can you tell me where there is a hotel?
Può dirmi Lei dov'è un buon ristorante?	Can you tell me where there is a good restaurant?
Può dirmi dov'è il telefono?[1]	Can you tell where the telephone is?
Può dirmi dov'è la stazione ferroviaria?	Can you tell me where the train station is?
Può dirmi dov'è l'ufficio postale?	Can you tell me where the post office is?

QUIZ 3

1. *Dov'è un albergo?* a. Where's the telphone?
2. *Dov'è il telefono?* b. Can you tell me where the train station is?
3. *Può dirmi Lei ...?* c. Can you tell me ...?
4. *Può dirmi dov'è la stazione ferroviaria?* d. the post office
5. *l'ufficio postale* e. Where is a hotel?

ANSWERS

1—e; 2—a; 3—c; 4—b; 5—d.

C. Do You Have ...?

Ha Lei ...?	Do you have ...?
Hai	Do you have... ? (*familiar*)
denaro	(any) money
sigarette	(any) cigarettes
fiammiferi	(any) matches

[1] Note that the quesiton Può dirmi... ? (Can you tell me?) can be used with or without the pronoun Lei.

Ho bisogno di ...	I need ...
carta	(some) paper
una matita	a pencil
una penna	a pen
un francobollo	a stamp
dentifricio	toothpaste
un asciugamano	a towel
sapone	soap
Dove posso comprare...?	Where can I buy...?
un dizionario italiano	an Italian dictionary
un dizionario inglese-italiano	an English-Italian dictionary
un libro in inglese	an English book
degli abiti	some clothes

D. In a Restaurant

prima colazione	breakfast
colazione	lunch
pranzo	dinner
cena	supper
Che cosa desidera?	What will you have? (What do you wish?)
Che cosa desidera mangiare?	What would you like to eat?
Mi dia il menu, per favore.	Give me the menu, please.
Posso avere il menu, per favore?	May I have a menu, please?
Mi porti ...	Bring me ...
un po' di pane	some bread
pane e burro	bread and butter
della minestra	some soup
della carne	some meat
del manzo	some beef

una bistecca	a steak
del prosciutto	some ham
del pesce	some fish
del pollo	some chicken
delle uova	some eggs
della verdura	some vegetables
delle patate	some potatoes
dell'insalata	some salad
dell'acqua	some water
del vino	some wine
della birra	some beer
del latte	some milk
caffelatte	coffee with milk
dello zucchero	some sugar
del sale	some salt
del pepe	some pepper
della frutta	some fruit
dei dolci	some dessert

Mi porti ... Bring me ...

una tazza di caffè	a cup of coffee
una tazza di tè	a cup of tea
un tovagliolo	a napkin
un cucchiaio	a spoon
un cucchiaino	a teaspoon
un coltello	a knife
un piatto	a plate
un bicchiere	a glass

Desidero ... I would like ...

un po' di frutta	some fruit (assorted)
una bottiglia di vino	a bottle of wine
un' altra bottiglia di vino	another bottle of wine
un po' di più	a little more
un po' più di pane	a little more bread
un po' più di carne	a little more meat
Il conto, per favore.	The check, please.

QUIZ 4

1. *carne*	a. fish
2. *patate*	b. water
3. *acqua*	c. vegetables
4. *Che cosa desidera?*	d. I need soap.
5. *uova*	e. The check, please.
6. *pollo*	f. breakfast
7. *pesce*	g. a spoon
8. *una bottiglia di vino*	h. coffee with milk
9. *Ho bisogno di sapone.*	i. What will you have?
10. *Mi porti un po' più dì pane.*	j. dessert
11. *caffelatte*	k. meat
12. *zucchero*	l. a knife
13. *verdura*	m. eggs
14. *una tazza di tè*	n. Bring me a little more bread.
15. *un piatto*	o. chicken
16. *un coltello*	p. a cup of tea
17. *dolci*	q. a plate
18. *prima colazione*	r. sugar
19. *un cucchiaio*	s. a bottle of wine
20. *Il conto, per favore.*	t. potatoes

ANSWERS

1—k; 2—t; 3—b; 4—i; 5—m; 6—o; 7—a; 8—s; 9—d; 10—n; 11—h; 12—r; 13—c; 14—p; 15—q; 16—l; 17—j; 18—f; 19—g; 20—e.

LESSON 8

A. TO SPEAK: *PARLARE*

io parlo	I speak
tu parli	you speak (*familiar*)
lui parla	he speaks
lei parla	she speaks
Lei parla	you speak (*polite*)
noi parliamo	we speak
voi parlate	you speak (*plural*)
loro parlano	they speak (*masc. or fem.*)
Loro parlano	you speak (*polite*)

NOTES

1. These forms, which make up the present tense, translate into the English as "I speak," "I am speaking" and "I do speak." *Parlare* is an *-are* verb (also called a verb of the first conjugation) because its infinitive form (to speak) ends in *-are*. There are many other common *-are* verbs that are conjugated like *parlare*.

lavorare	to work	**mangiare**	to eat
studiare	to study	**cucinare**	to cook

2. *Tu*, you, is used to address people you know very well (whom you call by their first names in English--relatives, close friends, children, pets, etc.) The plural for *tu* is *voi*. In Southern Italy *voi* is also used to address one or more persons as an intermediate form between the familiar *tu* and the polite *Lei*.
3. Notice that there are six endings that indicate the person speaking or spoken about, without need of pronouns:

Singular:

-o indicates the speaker (I)

-i indicates the person spoken to (you). It is used only with someone you know well.

-*a* indicates someone or something spoken about (he, she, it) or else you (*polite*).

Plural:

-*iamo* indicates several speakers (we).

-*ate* is the plural form for *tu. Voi* is also used to address one or more persons in a formal way.

-*ano* indicates they (both masculine and feminine) or the plural of the polite form.

4. Notice that the verb form with *Lei, lui, lei* is the same: *parla.*
5. Notice that *lui* or *lei* is used with the verb form *parla,* depending on whether you are referring to a man or a woman.

lui parla	he is speaking
lei parla	she is speaking

6. The subject pronouns *Lei, loro,* and the direct object pronouns *le, la, li* (you) are often capitalized to emphasize the idea of respect toward a person—for instance, when writing a formal letter or addressing someone in a respectful way. (They are capitalized in this program for clarity.)

B. THE AND A

1. The

MASCULINE

Singular:		Plural:	
il libro	the book	**i libri**	the books
lo studio	the study	**gli studi**	the studies
l'esercizio	the exercise	**gli esercizi**	the exercises

FEMININE

Singular:		Plural:	
la donna	the lady	**le donne**	the ladies
l'agenzia	the agency	**le agenzie**	the agencies

Notice the different forms used in Italian for the single

English word *the.* In Italian, words are either masculine or feminine. When they refer to males or females, you know which group of articles to use, but in the case of other nouns, you have to learn whether the noun is masculine or feminine. The masculine article *il* and its plural form *i* are used before masculine nouns beginning with a consonant. The masculine article *lo* and its plural form *gli* are used before masculine nouns beginning with a vowel or a *z,* or *s* plus a consonant, or the consonant combination *gn.* When used before a vowel, *lo* is elided to *l';* the plural does not elide unless the following word begins with an *i.* The feminine article *la* and its plural form *le* are used before feminine nouns; however, before vowels, they are also elided to *l'.*

2. A (An)

un ragazzo	a boy	**una ragazza**	a girl
uno zero	a zero	**un'amica**	a friend (*fem.*)

The indefinite article (a, an) has the form *un* before masculine nouns beginning with vowels and most consonants. It takes the form *uno* before masculine nouns beginning with consonant *z,* or *s* plus a consonant, or the combination *gn.* The feminine form is *una,* eliding to *un'* before a vowel.

QUIZ 5

1. *io*	a. they speak
2. *noi*	b. she is speaking
3. *tu parli*	c. she
4. *lui*	d. you (*fam. plur.*)
5. *loro parlano*	e. I
6. *voi*	f. you speak
7. *tu*	g. he
8. *lei*	h. we speak

9.	*noi parliamo*	i.	you (*fam. sing.*)
10.	*lei parla*	j.	we

ANSWERS

1—e; 2—j; 3—f; 4—g; 5—a; 6—d; 7—i; 8—c; 9—h; 10—b.

C. Contractions

di + il = del (of the)
di + lo = dello
di + la = della
di + l' = dell'
di + i = dei
di + gli = degli
di + le = delle

a + il = al (to the)
a + lo = allo
a + la = alla
a + l' = all'
a + i = ai
a + gli = agli
a + le = alle

con + il = col (with the)
con + i = coi

su + il = sul (on the)
su + la = sulla
su + lo = sullo
su + gli = sugli

D. Plural of Nouns

As a general rule, nouns ending in *o* are masculine, nouns ending in *a* are feminine, and nouns ending in *e* can be either masculine or feminine.

All masculine nouns (ending either in *o* or *e*) form their plural with an *i*.

Feminine nouns that end in *a* in the singular, form their plural with an *e*. Feminine nouns that end in *e* in the singular, form their plural with an *i*.

il piatto	the plate	**i piatti**	the plates
il cuore	the heart	**i cuori**	the hearts

la rosa	the rose	**le rose**	the roses
la valle	the valley	**le valli**	the valleys

E. Adjectives

There are two groups of adjectives:

1. Those that have four endings:

caro *(masc. sing.)* **cara** *(fem. sing.)*
cari *(masc. plur.)* **care** *(fem. plur.)*

2. Those that have only two endings

gentile *(masc. and fem. sing.)*
gentili *(masc. and fem. plur.)*

Study these examples:

un caro amico	a dear friend (*masc.*)
una cara amica	a dear friend (*fem.*)
dei cari amici	some dear friends (*masc.*)
delle care amiche	some dear friends (*fem.*)
un uomo gentile	a kind man (*masc.*)
una donna gentile	a kind woman (*fem.*)
degli uomini gentili[1]	some kind men (*masc.*)
delle donne gentili[1]	some kind women (*fem.*)

The adjective always agrees with its noun. When an adjective is used alone, its ending usually tells you whether it refers to a singular or plural, feminine or masculine noun:

È italiano.	He is Italian.
È italiana.	She is Italian.
Sono italiani.	They are Italian. (*masc.*)
Sono italiane.	They are Italian. (*fem.*)

[1] Note that some adjectives come before the noun they modify, and some after. See Position of the Adjective in the Summary of Italian Grammar.

NOTES

Only proper names and geographical nouns are capitalized in Italian. Names of nationalities are capitalized only when used as nouns and referring to a person. When used as adjectives, or to refer to a language, they are not capitalized.

Examples:

un libro italiano	an Italian book
Ho incontrato un Italiano.	I met an Italian.
Loro parlano l'italiano.	They speak Italian.

F. POSSESSION

English -*'s* or -*s'* is translated by *di* (of):

il libro di Giovanni	John's book (the book of John)
i libri dei ragazzi	the boys' books (the books of the boys)
il libro di Maria	Maria's book
i libri delle ragazze	the girls' books

G. ASKING A QUESTION

To ask a question you can either put the subject after the verb:

Ha mangiato Lei?	Have you eaten?

or preserve the same word order and raise your voice at the end of the sentence to show that it is a question:

Lei ha mangiato.	You have eaten.
Lei ha mangiato?	Have you eaten?

H. NOT

The word for "not" is *non.* It comes before the verb.

Non vedo Marco. I don't see Mark.

REVIEW QUIZ 1

1. *Buon* ________ (morning), *signora Rossi.*
   a. *domani*
   b. *giorno*
   c. *grazie*
2. *Può dirmi* ________ (where's) *l'ufficio postale?*
   a. *dov'è*
   b. *buono*
   c. *lì*
3. ________ (Bring me) *un po' di pane.*
   a. *Mangiare*
   b. *Sera*
   c. *Mi porti*
4. *caffelatte con* ________ (sugar)
   a. *tè*
   b. *vino*
   c. *zucchero*
5. *un po'* ________ (more) *di carne*
   a. *più*
   b. *tazza*
   c. ancora
6. *il sette* ________ (January)
   a. *marzo*
   b. *gennaio*
   c. *agosto*
7. ________ (Wednesday), *cinque settembre*
   a. *inverno*
   b. *sabato*
   c. *mercoledì*
8. ________ (How) *sta?*
   a. *Grazie*
   b. *Come*
   c. *Sera*

9. *Buona* ________ (night), *signorina Rossi.*
   a. *fino*
   b. *notte*
   c. *io*
10. *Desidero una bottiglia di* ________ (wine).
   a. *latte*
   b. *vino*
   c. *acqua*

ANSWERS

1—b; 2—a; 3—c; 4—c; 5—a; 6—b; 7—c; 8—b; 9—b; 10—b.

LESSON 9

A. May I Introduce ...?

Buon giorno.	Good morning.
Buon giorno, signore.	Good morning, sir.
Come sta?	How are you? (*polite*)
Molto bene, grazie e Lei? E Lei americano?	Very well, thanks, and how are you? Are you American?
Sì signore.	Yes, sir.
Parla Lei italiano?	Do you speak Italian?
Un poco.	A little.
La presento alla mia amica signorina Rossi.	I present you to my friend Miss Rossi.
Posso presentarLe mia amica, signorina Rossi.	May I introduce my friend, Miss Rossi?
Molto piacere di conoscerLa.	Pleased to meet you. (Much pleasure in knowing you.)
Felice di conoscerLa.	I'm glad (happy) to meet (know) you.
Il piacere è mio.	The pleasure is mine.
Mi permetta che mi presenti: Giovanni Rossi.	Permit me to introduce myself: John Rossi.

Mi permetta che mi presenti? Sono Giovanni Rossi.	May I introduce myself? I am John Rossi.

B. How Are Things?

Buon giorno, Paolo!	Hello, Paul!
Ciao, Giovanni!	Hello, John!
Come stai?	How are you? (*familiar*)
Come vanno le cose?	How are things? (How go things?)
Bene e tu?	Fine and how are you?
che c'è	what is there
di nuovo	(of) new
Che c'è di nuovo?	What's new?
niente	nothing
di particolare	in (of) particular
Niente di particolare.	Nothing in particular.
che	what
mi racconti	do (you) tell me
Che mi racconti?	What's new?
Poche cose.	(Little things) Not much.
Non molto.	Not much.

C. Good-Bye

È stato	It's been
un vero piacere.	a real pleasure.
È stato un vero piacere.	It's been a real pleasure.
Il piacere	the pleasure
Il piacere è stato mio.	The pleasure was mine.
Arrivederci ad un altro giorno.	Good-bye until another day.
A presto.	See you soon.
A più tardi.	Until later. See you soon.
Buona notte.	Good night.
Ciao!	Good-bye./Hello. (*familiar*)

A dopo!	See you later
Ci vediamo.	See you.
Alla prossima.	Until next (time).
A domani.	See you tomorrow.

QUIZ 6

1. *Come stai?*	a. Nothing in particular.
2. *Arrivederci.*	b. Allow me to introduce you to my friend.
3. *Buona notte.*	c. See you soon.
4. *Buon giorno, Giovanni.*	d. Hello, John.
5. *Niente di particolare.*	e. I'm very glad to know you.
6. *Mi permetta di presentarLa al mio amico.*	f. How are you?
7. *A presto.*	g. Good night.
8. *nuovo*	h. to meet you
9. *Molto piacere di conoscerLa*	i. new
10. *conoscerLa*	j. Good-bye.

ANSWERS

1—f; 2—j; 3—g; 4—d; 5—a; 6—b; 7—c; 8—i; 9—e; 10—h.

LESSON 10

A. To Be or Not To Be[1]: *Essere*

Study these forms of the important irregular verb *essere*, "to be."

io sono	I am
tu sei	you are *(familiar)*
Lei è	you are *(polite)*
lui è	he is
lei è	she is
noi siamo	we are
voi siete	you are *(familiar)*
Loro sono	you are *(polite plur.)*
loro sono	they are

Lui è dottore.	He is a doctor.
Lui è scrittore.	He is a writer.
Lui è italiano.	He's Italian.
Il libro è rosso.	The book is red.
Lei è giovane.	She is young.
Il ghiaccio è freddo.	Ice is cold.
Lui è intelligente.	He's intelligent.
Lei è incantevole.	She's charming.
Sono io.	It's I.
Di dov'è Lei?	Where are you from? *(formal)*
Di dov'è sei?	Where are you from? *(fam.)*
Io sono italiano.	I'm Italian.
Di quale è fatto?	What is it made of?
È fatto di legno.	It's made of wood.
È d'argento.	It's silver.
Di chi è questo?	Whose is this?
Il libro è del signor Rossi.	The book belongs to Mr. Rossi.

[1] See p. 226 of Grammar Summary for more information about *essere*.

È l'una.	It's one o'clock.
Sono le due.	It's two o'clock.
Sono le nove e dieci.	It's ten past nine.
Costano quindicimila lire la dozzina.	They are fifteen thousand lire a dozen.
Sono nove dollari l'uno.	They are nine dollars each.
È tardi.	It's late.
È presto.	It's early.
È necessario.	It's necessary.
È un peccato.	It's a pity.
Non è vero?	Right? (Isn't it true?)

Io sto	I stay (am)
tu stai	you stay (are)
lui sta	he stays (is)
noi stiamo	we stay (are)
voi state	you stay (are)
loro stanno	they stay (are)

Stare means to stay, to remain, but in certain expressions it can mean to be. For example in expressions of health:

Come sta?[1]	How are you? (*polite*)
Sto bene.	I am well.

QUIZ 7

1. *Lui è intelligente.* — a. Whose is this?
2. *È un peccato.* — b. Where are you from?
3. *Lui è dottore.* — c. They are.
4. *Io sono.* — d. He's a doctor.
5. *È l'una.* — e. It's early.
6. *Noi siamo.* — f. He's Italian.

1 See p. 238 for the verb *stare*.

7. *È fatto di legno.*
8. *Di dov'è Lei?*
9. *È presto.*
10. *Io sono stanco.*
11. *Loro sono.*
12. *Di chi è questo?*
13. *È tardi.*
14. *Lui è italiano.*

g. He's intelligent.
h. It's a pity.
i. I am.
j. It's one o'clock.
k. It's made of wood.
l. We are.
m. I'm tired.
n. It's late.

ANSWERS

1—g; 2—h; 3—d; 4—i; 5—j; 6—l; 7—k; 8—b; 9—e; 10—m; 11—c; 12—a; 13—n; 14—f.

B. It Is ...

È ...	It is ...
È vero.	It's true.
Questo non è vero.	That isn't true.
Questo non è così.	That isn't so.
È così. Così è.	It's so. That's the way it is.
È male.	It's bad.
È molto male.	It's very bad.
È certo.	It's certain.
È grande.	It's big.
È piccolo.	It's small.
È caro.	It's expensive.
È economico.	It's cheap.
È vicino.	It's near.
È lontano.	It's far.
È difficile.	It's difficult.
È facile.	It's easy.
È poco. Non è molto.	It's a little. It's not much.
È molto poco.	It's very little.
È molto.	It's a lot.

È abbastanza.	It's enough.
Non è abbastanza.	It's not enough.
È qui.	It's here.
È lì.	It's there.
È tuo.	It's yours. *(familiar)*
È Suo.	It's yours. *(polite)*
È mio.	It's mine.
È nostro.	It's ours.
È per te.	It's for you. *(familiar)*
È per Lei.	It's for you. *(polite)*

QUIZ 8

1. *È molto.* — a. It's enough.
2. *È facile.* — b. That isn't true.
3. *È vicino.* — c. It's bad.
4. *È abbastanza.* — d. It's near.
5. *Questo non è vero.* — e. It's mine.
6. *È male.* — f. It's true.
7. *È piccolo.* — g. It's here.
8. *È vero.* — h. It's small.
9. *È mio.* — i. It's easy.
10. *È qui.* — j. It's a lot.

ANSWERS

1—j; 2—i; 3—d; 4—a; 5—b; 6—c; 7—h; 8—f; 9—e; 10—g.

C. To Have and Have Not: *Avere*

TO HAVE

io ho	I have
tu hai	you have *(familiar)*
Lei ha	you have *(polite)*

lui ha	he has
noi abbiamo	we have
voi avete	you have
loro hanno	they have

NOT TO HAVE

io non ho	I don't have
tu non hai	you don't have *(familiar)*
Lei non ha	you don't have *(polite)*
lui non ha	he doesn't have
noi non abbiamo	we don't have
voi non avete	you don't have
loro non hanno	they don't have

Study these expressions with *avere.*

Io ho tempo.	I have time.
Io non ho tempo.	I haven't any time.
Lui non ha amici.	He doesn't have any friends.
Ha Lei una sigaretta?	Do you have a cigarette?
Io ho fame.	I'm hungry. (I have hunger.)
Ho sete. (Io ho sete.)	I'm thirsty. (I have thirst.)
Ho freddo. (Io ho freddo.)	I'm cold. (I have cold.)
Ho caldo (Io ho caldo.)	I'm warm. (I have warmth.)
Ho ragione.	I'm right. (I have reason.)

QUIZ 9

1. *Noi Abbiamo*	a. I'm cold.
2. *Lui non ha.*	b. We have.
3. *Io non ho tempo.*	c. He doesn't have.
4. *Ho freddo.*	d. I'm hungry.
5. *Io ho fame.*	e. I don't have time.

ANSWERS

1—b; 2—c; 3—e; 4—a; 5—d.

LESSON 11

A. I Only Know a Little Italian.

1. *Parlare:* to speak

Parla italiano?	Do you speak Italian?
Parla Lei italiano?	
Sì, un poco.	Yes, a little.
Molto poco.	Very little.
Non molto bene.	Not very well.
Io parlo italiano.	I speak Italian.
Lo parlo male.	I speak it poorly.
Io non lo parlo molto bene.	I don't speak it very well.

2. *Conoscere:* to know

Io conosco solo poche parole.	I know only a few words.
Lo leggo ma non lo parlo.	I read it, but I don't speak it.

3. *Leggere:* to read; *Dire:* to say

Che cosa ha detto?	What did you say?
Il suo amico parla italiano?	Does your friend speak Italian?
No il mio amico non parla italiano.	No, my friend doesn't speak Italian.

4. *Capire; comprendere:* to understand

Capisce l'italiano?	Do you understand Italian?
Sì, capisco italiano.	Yes, I understand Italian.
Lo capisco ma non lo parlo.	I understand it, but I don't speak it.

Lo leggo ma non lo parlo.	I read it, but I don't speak it.
No, io non capisco l'italiano.	No, I don't understand Italian.
Io non capisco molto bene l'italiano.	I don't understand Italian very well.
Non lo pronuncio molto bene.	I don't pronounce it very well.
Mi manca la pratica.	I lack practice.
Ho bisogno di pratica.	I need practice.
Lei mi comprende?	Do you understand me?
Io la comprendo.	I understand you.
Io non la comprendo molto bene.	I don't understand you very well.
Lei parla troppo in fretta.	You speak too fast. (You speak in too much of a hurry.)
Lei parla troppo veloce.	You are speaking too fast.
Non parli così in fretta.	Don't speak so fast.
Parli più lentamente.	Speak more slowly.
Per favore parli più lentamente.	Please speak a little more slowly.
Mi scusi ma non La capisco. Non L'ho capita.	Excuse me, but I don't understand. I didn't understand you.
Per favore me lo ripeta.	Please say it again (to me).
Mi comprende ora?	Do you understand me now?
Oh, ora capisco.	Oh, now I understand.

5. *Scrivere:* to write; *Significare:* to denote

Che cosa significa in italiano?	What does that mean in Italian?
Come si dice "Thanks" in italiano?	How do you say "Thanks" in Italian?
Come si scrive questa parola?	How do you spell (write) that word?
Per favore me la scriva.	Please write it down for me.

B. A Brief Conversation with a Stranger

Buon giorno, signore.	Good morning, sir.
Buon giorno.	Good morning.
Lei parla italiano?	Do you speak Italian?
Sì, io parlo italiano.	Yes, I speak Italian.
Io non parlo inglese.	I don't speak English.
È Lei italiano?	Are you Italian?
Sì, io sono italiano.	Yes, I am Italian.
Da quanto tempo è Lei negli Stati Uniti?	How long have you been in the United States?
Da tre mesi.	For three months.
Lei imparerà presto l'inglese.	You'll soon learn English.
Lei imparerà l'inglese in poco tempo. Non è molto difficile.	You'll learn English in a short time. It's not very hard.
È più difficile di quanto creda.	It's harder than you think.
Forse lei ha ragione.	You are probably right.
È più facile per noi imparare l'italiano che per voi l'inglese.	It is easier for us to learn Italian than for you (to learn) English.
Lei parla italiano molto bene.	You speak Italian very well.
Io ho vissuto in Italia per diversi anni.	I lived in Italy for several years.
Lei ha un'ottima pronuncia.	You have (an) excellent pronunciation.
Molte grazie, ma mi manca la pratica.	Thank you, but I need (lack) practice.
Ho bisogno di pratica.	I need practice.
Adesso devo andare. Il mio treno sta per partire.	I have to leave now. My train's about to leave.
Buona fortuna e buon viaggio.	Good luck and a pleasant trip.
Altrettanto.	The same to you.
Addio.	Good-bye.

C. Excuse Me and Thank You

Mi scusi.	Pardon me. Excuse me.
Le chiedo scusa.	I beg your pardon.
Per favore, ripeta.	Please repeat.
Mi vuole fare il favore di reipetere?	Will you do me the favor of repeating it?
Con piacere.	With pleasure. Gladly.
Con molto piacere.	With the greatest pleasure.
Sono a Sua disposizione.	I'm at your disposal.
Che cosa posso fare per Lei?	What (thing) can I do for you?
Lei è molto gentile.	You are very kind.
Lei è molto cortese.	You are very kind. (You are very courteous.)
Grazie.	Thanks.
Molte grazie.	Many thanks.
Grazie infinite.	Thanks a lot. (Infinite thanks.)
Mille grazie.	Thanks very much. (A thousand thanks.)
Di niente.	Don't mention it. (Of nothing.)
Non c'è di che.	Don't mention it.
Niente affatto.	It's nothing. (Nothing at all.)

QUIZ 10

1. *Lo comprendo ma non lo parlo.*	a. Do you speak Italian?
2. *Mi comprende ora?*	b. I need practice.
3. *Non lo parlo molto bene*	c. Don't mention it.
4. *Lei è molto gentile.*	d. What did you say?
5. *Come si scrive questa parola?*	e. Say it again.
6. *Lei parla italiano?*	f. Not very well.
7. *Ho bisogno di practica.*	g. I didn't understand very well.

8. *Non c'è di che.*	h. I understand it, but I don't speak it.
9. *Me lo ripeta.*	i. Speak more slowly.
10. *Non molto bene.*	j. I don't speak it very well.
11. *Parli più lentamente.*	k. How do you say "Thanks" in Italian?
12. *Mille grazie.*	l. You are very kind.
13. *Che cosa ha detto?*	m. Do you understand me now?
14. *Come si dice "Thanks" in italiano?*	n. How do you spell this word?
15. *Non ho capito bene.*	o. Thank you very much.

ANSWERS

1—h; 2—m; 3—j; 4—l; 5—n; 6—a; 7—b; 8—c; 9—e; 10—f; 11—i; 12—o; 13—d; 14—k; 15—g.

D. Word Study

commedia	comedy
costante	constant
contrario	contrary
desiderio	desire
lungo	long
opera	opera
semplice	simple
venditore	vendor

LESSON 12

A. This and That (Demonstrative Pronouns and Adjectives)

Study the following expressions using the domonstratives *questo* and *quello*.[1]

Dammi questo.	Give me this one. (*masc.*)
Dammi questa.	Give me this one. (*fem.*)
Dammi questi.	Give me these. (*masc.*)
Dammi queste.	Give me these. (*fem.*)
Dammi quello.	Give me that one. (*masc.*)
Dammi quella.	Give me that one. (*fem.*)
Dammi quelli.	Give me those. (*masc.*)
Dammi quelle.	Give me those. (*fem.*)
Dammi quello là.	Give me that one (*masc.*) over there.
Dammi quella là.	Give me that one (*fem.*) over there.
Dammi quelli là.	Give me those (*masc.*) over there.
Dammi quelle là.	Give me those (*fem.*) over there.

When *questo* and *quello* are used as adjectives preceding nouns, the forms of *questo* are as above, but *quello* has a different set of endings:

questo ragazzo	this boy
questa signora	this lady
quel signore là	that gentleman over there
quella signora	that lady
quello sbaglio	that mistake
quei vicini	those neighbors
quegli studenti	those students

[1] See also Demonstratives in the Summary of Italian Grammar.

QUIZ 11

1. *Dammi questi.*
2. *questo*
3. *Dammi quella.*
4. *questo ragazzo*
5. *quello*
6. *quei vicini*
7. *Dammi quelli là.*
8. *quello là*
9. *questa signora*
10. *quel signore là*

a. Give me those over there.
b. that one over there
c. this lady
d. this one
e. that gentleman over there
f. this boy
g. Give me these.
h. that one
i. those neighbors
j. Give me that one. (*fem.*)

ANSWERS

1—g; 2—d; 3—j; 4—f; 5—h; 6—i; 7—a; 8—b; 9—c; 10—e.

B. More or Less

1. More

più piano more slowly
più difficile more difficult
più facile easier
più lontano farther
più vicino nearer
più di quello more than that
più di un anno more than a year

2. Less

meno piano less slowly
meno difficile less difficult
meno facile less easy
meno lontano less far, not so far

meno vicino	less near, not so near
meno di quello	less than that
meno di un anno	less than a year

C. And, Or, But

1. *e* "and"

Roberto e Giovanni sono fratelli.	Robert and John are brothers.

ed is used instead of *e* before nouns beginning with a vowel:

Roberto ed Andrea sono fratelli.	Robert and Andrew are brothers.

2. *o* "or"

cinque o sei lire	five or six lire
sette o otto ore	seven or eight hours

3. *ma* "but"

Lui non è francese ma inglese.	He is not French but English.
Lui non viene oggi ma domani.	He is not coming today but tomorrow.

D. Word Study

catena	chain
lettera	letter
completo	complete
crèare	create
eterno	eternal
fontana	fountain
ufficiale	officer

QUIZ 12

1. *inglese*	a. five or six days
2. *e*	b. more than that
3. *ma*	c. seven or eight hours
4. *più facile*	d. English
5. *fratello*	e. but
6. *cinque o sei giorni*	f. tomorrow
7. *meno piano*	g. easier
8. *più di quello*	h. and
9. *domani*	i. less slowly
10. *sette o otto ore*	j. brother

ANSWERS

1—d; 2—h; 3—e; 4—g; 5—j; 6—a; 7—i; 8—b; 9—f; 10—c.

LESSON 13

A. Where?

Dove?	Where?
Dov'è?	Where is it?
Dove si trova?	Where is it found?
Qui.	Here.
Lì.	There.
All'angolo.	On the corner.
È in via Condotti.	It's on the Via Condotti. (*via* = street)
Si trova in via Condotti.[1]	It's found on the via Condotti.

[1] *È* and *si trova* are two interchangeable ways of telling the location of something.

D. Near and Far

qui vicino	near here
molto vicino	very near
a pochi passi da qui	a few steps from here
vicino al paese	near the town
vicino al parco	near the park
vicino alla chiesa	next to the church
È lontano?	Is it far?
È lontano da qui?	Is it far from here?
È più lontano.	It's farther.
È un po' più lontano.	It's a little farther.
Quanto è lontano da qui?	How far is it from here?
È vicino.	It's near.
Non è troppo lontano.	It's not too far.
È lontano da qui?	Is it far from here?
È molto lontano.	It's very far.
Non è molto lontano.	It's not too far.
Si trova a duecento metri da qui.	It's two hundred meters from here.
È a un chilometro da qui.	It's a kilometer from here.

QUIZ 13

1. *lì in Italia*	a. I expect to see him there.
2. *Mi aspetti qui.*	b. in there
3. *qui*	c. to the left
4. *a destra*	d. It's far.
5. *lì*	e. here
6. *È proprio qui.*	f. Wait for me here.
7. *Io spero di vederlo lì.*	g. straight ahead
8. *a sinistra*	h. to the right
9. *È lontano.*	i. there

10. *lì dentro* — j. Go there.

11. *È lì, da qualche parte.* — k. Go that way.

12. *È vicino.* — l. It's right here.

13. *Vada lì.* — m. over there in Italy

14. *Vada per quella strada.* — n. It's somewhere around there.

15. *sempre avanti* — o. It's near.

ANSWERS

1—m; 2—f; 3—e; 4—h; 5—i; 6—l; 7—a; 8—c; 9—d; 10—b; 11—n; 12—o; 13—j; 14—k; 15—g.

REVIEW QUIZ 2

1. ________ (this) *ragazzo*
   a. *questa*
   b. *questo*
   c. *queste*
2. *Dammi* ________ (those, *fem.*).
   a. *quelle*
   b. *queste*
   c. *questo*
3. *Ho* ________ (here) *i libri*.
   a. *lui*
   b. *qui*
   c. *come*
4. *Venga* ________ (here).
   a. *lei*
   b. *lì*
   c. *qui*
5. *Domani vado* ________ (there).
   a. *lì*
   b. *noi*
   c. *come*

6. ________ (Where) *sta?*
   a. *Là*
   b. *Dove*
   c. *Qui*
7. *È* ________ (far) *da qui?*
   a. *lontano*
   b. *quella*
   c. *lì*
8. *Roberto* ________ (and) *Giovanni sono fratelli.*
   a. *con*
   b. *e*
   c. *più*
9. *cinque* ________ (or) *sei lire*
   a. *o*
   b. *e*
   c. *più*
10. *Desidero venire* ________ (but) *non posso.*
   a. *o*
   b. *ma*
   c. *fino*

ANSWERS

1—b; 2—a; 3—b; 4—c; 5—a; 6—b; 7—a; 8—b; 9—a; 10—b.

LESSON 14

A. I, You, He, etc. (Subject Pronouns)

The use of the subject pronouns is optional: "I speak" is just *parlo*; "we speak," *parliamo*; etc. But the pronouns are used for emphasis or clearness:

Io studio, tu ti diverti.	I study, you enjoy yourself.
La signora pensa che io goda buona salute.	The lady thinks that I enjoy good health.

SINGULAR

I, You, He, She

io	I
tu	you (*familiar*)
lui	he
lei	she
Lei	you (*polite*)
io parlo	I speak
tu parli	you speak (*familiar*)
lui parla	he speaks
lei parla	she speaks
Lei parla	you speak (*polite*)

PLURAL

We, You, They

noi	we
voi	you
loro	they (*masc.*)
loro	they (*fem.*)
Loro	they, you (*polite*)
noi parliamo	we speak
voi parlate	you speak (*fam. plur.; polite*)
loro parlano	they speak
loro parlano	they speak (*fem.*)
Loro parlano	they speak, you speak (*polite*)

B. It's Me (I), You, He, etc.

Sono io.	It's I.
Sei tu.	It's you (*familiar*)
È lui.	It's he.
È lei.	It's she.
Siamo noi.	It's we.
Siete voi.	It's you (*familiar*)
Sono loro.	It's they. It's you. (*polite plur.*)

C. It and Them (Direct Object Pronouns)

	SINGULAR,		PLURAL	
MASCULINE	*lo*	it	***li***	them
FEMININE	*la*	it	***le***	them

Ha il denaro?	Do you have the money?
Sì ce l'ho.[1]	Yes I have it.
Ha la borsetta?	Do you have the handbag?
Sì, ce l'ho.[1]	Yes, I have it.
Ha visto Pietro e Giovanni?	Have you seen Peter and John?
Sì, io li ho visti.	Yes, I have seen them.
Ha visto Maria e Luisa?	Have you seen Mary and Louise?
Sì, io le ho viste.	Yes, I saw them.

Notice that the pronoun agrees with the word it refers to. *Lo* and *la* elide; *li* and *le* do not. *Lo* is used when the reference is to an idea or a whole expression:

Lo capisco.	I understand it.

Lo, la, etc. usually come immediately before the verb, as in the case of other object pronouns. However, they are added to the infinitive:

Voglio capirlo.	I want to understand it.

D. Word Study

banda	band
composizione	compostion
coscienza	conscience
decorazione	decoration
descrizione	description
missione	mission

[1] *Lo* and *la* elide to *l'* before vowel sounds.

numero	number
ottimista	optimist
regione	region

LESSON 15

A. MY, YOUR, HIS/HER, ETC. (POSSESSIVE ADJECTIVES)

mio, -a, -ei, -e	my
tuo, -a, -oi, -e	your (*fam.*)
suo, -a, -oi, -e	his, her, your (*polite*)
nostro, -a, -i, -e	our
vostro, -a, -i, -e	your (*fam. pl.*)
loro	their, your (*polite pl.*)

In Italian the possessive adjective is always preceded by the definite article, except when it comes before members of the family in the singular. *Loro* is always preceded by the article.

tuo fratello	your brother
mia figlia	my sister
il loro figlio	their son

Study the following examples:

SINGULAR

il mio amico	my friend *(masc.)*
la mia amica[1]	my friend *(fem.)*
il tuo amico	your friend
il Suo amico	his, her, your friend

[1] Note that the possessive adjective agrees in gender with the noun that follows rather than with the subject: *la mia amica* = my (female) friend. The speaker may be male or female

il nostro amico	our friend
la nostra amica	our friend
il vostro amico	your friend
la vostra amica	your friend
il Loro amico	their friend, your friend

PLURAL

i miei amici	my friends
i tuoi amici	your friends
i Suoi amici	your friends (*polite*)
i nostri amici	our friends
le nostre amiche	our friends (*fem.*)
i vostri amici	your friends
le vostre amiche	your friends (*fem.*)
i Loro amici	your friends (*polite*)

SINGULAR

il mio cappello	my hat
il tuo vestito	your dress
il suo vestito	her dress
il nostro amico	our friend
la nostra borsa	our bag
il vostro cavallo	your horse
la vostra penna	your pen

PLURAL

i miei cappelli	my hats
i tuoi vestiti	your dresses
i suoi vestiti	her dresses
i nostri amici	our friends
le nostre borse	our bags
i vostri cavalli	your horses
le vostre penne	your pens

B. It's Mine, Yours, His, etc. (Possessive Pronouns)

È mio, mia, etc.[1]	It's mine.
È tuo.	It's yours. (*fam.*)
È Suo.	It's yours. (*polite*)
È nostro.	It's ours.
È vostro.	It's yours.
È il loro.	It's theirs.
È il mio.	It's mine.
È il tuo.	It's yours.
È il Suo.	It's yours. (*polite*)
È il nostro.	It's ours.
È il vostro.	It's yours.
È il loro.	It's theirs.

Other examples:

i miei amici ed i tuoi	my friends and yours
Il suo libro è migliore del nostro.	His book is better than ours.

Generally the article is used with the possessive; however, in some cases it is omitted.

Di chi è questa lettera?	Whose is this letter?
È sua.	It's his.

C. To/For/About Me, You, Him, etc. (Prepositional Pronouns)

Notice the form of the pronoun when it comes after a preposition (see p. 207 for more prepositions):

[1] As with possessive adjectives, the gender of possessive pronouns depends on the noun they are replacing rather than the gender of the speaker.

per me	for me
per te	for you
con lui	with him
a lei	to her
a te	for you
senza noi	without us
con voi	with you
per loro	for them (*masc.*)
per loro	for them (*fem.*)
di voi	of, about you

Io parlo di te.	I'm speaking about you.
Marco va senza noi.	Mark is going without us.
Vuole andare con me.	He wants to go with me.
Lei parla di lui.	She is speaking about him.
Scrivono a voi.	They write to you.

D. Direct and Indirect Object Pronouns

1. Direct object pronouns take the place of the direct object in a sentence; they receive the action of the verb. On page 53 *lo/la* and *li/le* (it and them) appeared; the following group of phrases shows all the direct object pronouns:

a. He sees me, you, him, etc.

Lui mi vede.	He sees me.
Lui ti vede.	He sees you. (*familiar*)
Io lo vedo.	I see him.
Io la vedo.	I see her.
Io La vedo.	I see you. (*polite*)
Loro ci vedono.	They see us.
Noi vi vediamo.	We see you. (*fam. pl.*)
Noi li vediamo.	We see them. (*masc.*)
Noi le vediamo.	We see them. (*fem.*)
Noi Li vediamo.	We see you. (*polite*)

b. She buys it.

Maria lo compra.	Maria buys it (a *masc. sing.* noun).
Maria la compra.	Maria buys it (a *fem. sing.* noun).
Maria li compra.	Maria buys them (a *masc. plur.* noun).
Maria le compra.	Maria buys them (a *fem. plur.* noun).

2. Indirect object pronouns indicate the person to, for, or from whom any action occurs, and they are the ultimate recipients of the verb's action. (In English, you sometimes use "to" before the indirect object pronoun.) Study these phrases:

a. He tells me ...

Lui mi dice ...	He tells me.
Lui ti dice ...	He tells you. (*fam. sing.*)
Lui gli dice ...	He tells him.
Lui le dice ...	He tells her.
Lui ci dice ...	He tells us.
Lui vi dice ...	He tells you.
Lui dice loro ...	He tells them.

b. I'm speaking to you.

Io le parlo.	I'm speaking to you. (*polite*)
Lui ti parla.	He is speaking to you.
Lui le parla.	He is speaking to you. (*polite*)

3. When there are two object pronouns in a sentence, the indirect precedes the direct, and both precede the conjugated verb[1]:

a. He gives it to me.

Lui me lo dà.	He gives it to me.
Lui te lo dà.	He gives it to you.
Lui glielo dà.	He gives it to him

[1] See also Position of Pronouns in the Summary of Italian Grammar.

Lui glielo dà.	He gives it to her.
Lui ce lo dà.	He gives it to us.
Lui ve lo dà.	He gives it to you.
Lui lo dà loro.	He gives it to them.

Notice the change in the form of some of the pronouns according to their position in the sentence.

E. Myself, Yourself, Himself, etc. (Reflexive Pronouns)

1. Notice the forms for "myself," "yourself," etc.: *mi, ti, si,* etc. Verbs that take these "reflexive pronouns" are called "reflexive" verbs.

Io mi lavo.	I wash myself. I get washed.
Tu ti lavi.	You wash yourself. You get washed.
Lui si lava.	He washes himself.
Lei si lava.	She washes herself.
Lei si lava.	You wash yourself. (*polite*)
Noi ci laviamo.	We wash ourselves.
Voi vi lavate.	You wash yourselves.
Loro si lavano.	They wash themselves.

Other examples:

Come si chiama?	What's your name? (How do you call yourself?)
Noi ci vediamo nello specchio.	We see ourselves in the mirror.
Loro si scrivono.	They write to one another.

2. Many verbs that are reflexive in Italian are not in English:

Mi diverto.	I'm having a good time.
Mi siedo.	I sit down. I'm sitting down.

Mi alzo.	I get up. I'm getting up (standing up).
Mi dimentico.	I forget.
Mi ricordo.	I remember.
Mi fermo.	I stop.
M'addormento.	I fall asleep.
Mi sbaglio.	I'm mistaken.

3. In Italian you don't say "I'm washing my hands," but "I'm washing the hands"; not "Take your hat off," but "Take off the hat":

Io mi lavo le mani.	I'm washing my hands.
Si tolga il cappello.	Take your hat off.
Lui si è rotto il braccio.	He broke (has broken) his arm.
Lei si è tagliato il dito.	She's cut her finger.
Mi sono fatto male alla mano.	I've hurt my hand.
Mi fa male la testa.	I have a headache.
Ho mal di testa.	
Mi fa male lo stomaco.	I have a stomachache.
Ho mal di stomaco.	
Sto perdendo la pazienza.	I'm losing my patience.

4. The reflexive forms are often used where we would use the passive in English:

Qui si parla italiano.	Italian is spoken here.
Le porte si aprono alle otto.	The doors open at eight.

The reflexive forms are also often used to translate our "one," "they," "people," etc.

Si dice che ...	It's said that ... People say that ... They say that ...
Qui si mangia bene.	The food's good here. (One eats well here.)

QUIZ 14

1.	*Mi siedo.*	a.	I get up.
2.	*M'addormento.*	b.	I stop.
3.	*Mi diverto.*	c.	I forget.
4.	*Mi ricordo.*	d.	I'm mistaken.
5.	*Mi alzo.*	e.	I wash myself.
6.	*Mi lavo.*	f.	I'm having a good time.
7.	*Mi sbaglio.*	g.	They write to each other.
8.	*Si scrivono.*	h.	I remember.
9.	*Mi dimentico.*	i.	I fall asleep.
10.	*Mi fermo.*	j.	I sit down.

ANSWERS

1—j; 2—i; 3—f; 4—h; 5—a; 6—e; 7—d; 8—g; 9—c; 10—b.

REVIEW QUIZ 3

1. *È* ________ (he).
   a. *lei*
   b. *lui*
   c. *io*
2. *Siamo* ________ (we).
   a. *loro*
   b. *tu*
   c. *noi*
3. *Io do il libro a* ________ (him).
   a. *lui*
   b. *voi*
   c. *loro*
4. *il* ________ (her) *vestito*
   a. *suo*
   b. *mio*
   c. *nostro*

5. *la* ________ (our) *carta*
   a. *nostro*
   b. *nostra*
   c. *tuo*
6 . *Dove sono i* ________ (my) *libri?*
   a. *tuoi*
   b. *miei*
   c. *nostri*
7. *Il suo libro è migliore del* ________ (ours).
   a. *tuoi*
   b. *nostro*
   c. *suoi*
8. *Parliamo di* ________ (him).
   a. *te*
   b. *loro*
   c. *lui*
9. *Lui* ________ (to us) *lo dice.*
   a. *lui*
   b. *ce*
   c. *voi*
10. *Come si* ________ (call) *lei?*
   a. *lava*
   b. *chiama*
   c. *vede*
11. *Noi ci* ________ (wash).
   a. *lava*
   b. *lavano*
   c. *laviamo*
12. *Mi* ________ (to be mistaken).
   a. *sbaglio*
   b. *lavo*
   c. *giro*
13. *Mi* ________ (sit down).
   a. *vado*
   b. *ricordo*
   c. *siedo*
14. *Mi sono* ________ (hurt) *alla mano.*
   a. *sbagliato*
   b. *lavo*
   c. *fatto male*

15. *Qui* ________ (is spoken). *italiano.*
   a. *si parla*
   b. *si mangia*
   c. *si chiamo*

ANSWERS

1—b; 2—c; 3—a; 4—a; 5—b; 6—b; 7—b; 8—c; 9—b; 10—b; 11—c; 12—a; 13—c; 14—c; 15—a.

LESSON 16

A. Some Action Phrases

Stia attento! Attenzione!	Watch out!
Faccia attenzione! Attento!	Be careful! Watch out!
Presto!	Fast! Hurry up!
Vada presto! Corra!	Go fast! Run!
Più presto!	Faster!
Non tanto di corsa.	Not so fast. (Don't run so much.)
Non molto in fretta.	Not very fast. Not in a hurry.
Non di corsa.	
Più piano. Senza fretta.	Slower. With no hurry.
Meno in fretta.	Slower.
Vengo. Io vengo. Sto venendo.	I'm coming.
Vengo subito. Corro.	I'm coming right away.
Corra. Faccia presto.	Hurry up.
Non c'è fretta. Non corra.	Don't hurry.
Io ho fretta.	I'm in a hurry.
Non ho fretta *(io)*.	I'm not in a hurry.
Un momento!	Just a minute! In a minute!
Al volo. Subito.	Right away.
Immediatamente.	Immediately.
Venga subito! Corra!	Come right away.
Presto.	Soon.

Immediatamente.	Immediately.
Più presto.	Sooner.
Più tardi.	Later.

B. May I Ask ...?

Posso farLe una domanda?	May I ask you a question?
Posso domandarLe ...? **Posso chiederLe ...?**	May I ask (you) ...?
Puó dirmi?	Can you tell me?
Potrebbe dirmi?	Could you tell me?
Mi vuol dire?	Will you tell me?
Potrebbe dirmi, per favore? **Vuol farmi il piacere di dirmi?**	Could you please tell me?
Che cosa vuol dire?	What do you mean?
Io voglio dire che ...	I mean that ...
Che cosa significa questo?	What does that mean?
Questo significa ...	This means ...

C. Word Study

destinazione	destination
diversione	diversion
liquido	liquid
obbligazione	obligation
occupazione	occupation
popolare	popular
solido	solid
teatro	theater

QUIZ 15

1.	*Stia attento! Attenozione!*	a.	Will you tell me?
2.	*Io ho fretta.*	b.	Right away.
3.	*Io voglio dire che . . .*	c.	Come right away!
4.	*Presto.*	d.	I'm coming!
5.	*Che cosa significa questo?*	e.	Watch out!
6.	*Più tardi.*	f.	Later.
7.	*Mi vuol dire?*	g.	I'm in a hurry.
8.	*Venga! Sto venendo!*	h.	I want to say that . . .
9.	*Venga subito! Corra!*	i.	What does this mean?
10.	*All'istante. Subito.*	j.	Soon.

ANSWERS

1—e; 2—g; 3—h; 4—j; 5—i; 6—f; 7—a; 8—d; 9—c; 10—b.

LESSON 17

A. Numbers

uno	one
due	two
tre	three
quattro	four
cinque	five
sei	six
sette	seven
otto	eight
nove	nine
dieci	ten

undici	eleven
dodici	twelve
tredici	thirteen
quattordici	fourteen
quindici	fifteen
sedici	sixteen
diciassette	seventeen
diciotto	eighteen
diciannove	nineteen
venti	twenty
ventuno	twenty-one
ventidue	twenty-two
ventitrè	twenty-three
trenta	thirty
trentuno	thirty-one
trentadue	thirty-two
trentatrè	thirty-three
quaranta	forty
quarantuno	forty-one
quarantadue	forty-two
quarantatrè	forty-three
cinquanta	fifty
cinquantuno	fifty-one
cinquantadue	fifty-two
cinquantatrè	fifty-three
sessanta	sixty
sessantuno	sixty-one
sessantadue	sixty-two
sessantatrè	sixty-three
settanta	seventy
settantuno	seventy-one
settantadue	seventy-two
settantatrè	seventy-three
ottanta	eighty
ottantuno	eighty-one
ottantadue	eighty-two
ottantatrè	eighty-three

novanta	ninety
novantuno	ninety-one
novantadue	ninety-two
novantatrè	ninety-three
cento	hundred
centouno	a hundred and one
centodue	a hundred and two
centotrè	a hundred and three
mille	thousand
milledue	a thousand and two
milletrè	a thousand and three

B. More Numbers

centoventi	120
centoventidue	122
centotrenta	130
centoquaranta	140
centocinquanta	150
centosessanta	160
centosettanta	170
centosettantuno	171
centosettantotto	178
centoottanta	180
centoottantadue	182
centonovanta	190
centonovantotto	198
centonovantanove	199
duecento	200
trecentoventiquattro	324
ottocentosettantacinque	875

primo	*-a, -i, -e*	first
secondo	*-a, -i, -e*	second
terzo	*-a, -i, -e*	third
quarto	*-a, -i, -e*	fourth

quinto	*-a, -i, -e*	fifth
sesto	*-a, -i, -e*	sixth
settimo	*-a, -i, -e*	seventh
ottavo	*-a, -i, -e*	eighth
nono	*-a, -i, -e*	ninth
decimo	*-a, -i, -e*	tenth

due e due fanno quattro	two and two are four
due più due fanno quattro	two and two are four
quattro più due fanno sei	four and two are six
dieci meno due fanno otto	ten minus two is eight

C. Word Study

amministrazione	administration
carattere	character
curioso	curious
tenda	curtain
dizionario	dictionary
grado	degree
ufficiale	official
piatto	plate

QUIZ 16

1. *mille*	a. 1,002
2. *undici*	b. 32
3. *cento*	c. 102
4. *diciassette*	d. 324
5. *trenta*	e. 11
6. *venti*	f. 1,000
7. *sessanta*	g. 60
8. *trecento ventiquattro*	h. 71
9. *trentadue*	i. 17
10. *centodue*	j. 875

11. *ottocento settantacinque* k. 83

12. *settantuno* l. 93

13. *mille e due* m. 20

14. *novantatrè* n. 30

15. *ottantatrè* o. 100

ANSWERS

1—f; 2—e; 3—o; 4—i; 5—n; 6—m; 7—g; 8—d; 9—b; 10—c; 11—j; 12—h; 13—a; 14—l; 15—k.

LESSON 18

A. How Much?

Quanto costa questo?	How much does this cost?
Costa quaranta lire.	It costs forty lire.
Quanto costa una libbra di caffe?	How much is a pound of coffee?
Costa cinquecento lire.	It costs 500 lire.

B. It Costs...

Costa ...	It costs ...
Questo libro costa duecento lire.	This book costs 200 lire.
Lui ha comprato un automobile per duemila dollari.	He bought a car for two thousand dollars.
Il viaggio in treno da Roma a Milano costa seimila lire.	The trip by train from Rome to Milan costs six thousand lire.
Ho risparmiato ventidue dollari per comprarmi un abito.	I've saved twenty-two dollars to buy a suit.

Lui ha guadagnato nel mese di giugno cinquemila-ottocentotrentaquattro lire.	He made 5,834 lire in the month of June.
Si vende solamente alla libbra e costa trecento lire.	It's sold only by the pound and costs 300 lire.

C. My Address Is ...

Io abito in via Nazionale, al numero duecento cinquanta.	I live at 250 Nazionale Street.
Lei abita al corso Italia numero trecento.	She lives at 300 Corso d'Italia.
Il negozio si trova in viale Mazzini, al numero trecentoventisei.	The store is at 326 Mazzini Avenue.
Loro si sono trasferiti in piazza Veneziano, al numero novecento-ventuno.	They moved to 921Venezia Square.

D. My Telephone Number Is...

Il mio numero di telefono è sei tre due otto otto.	My telephone number is 63288.
Il loro numero di telefono è quattro zero otto sei zero.	Their telephone number is 40860.
Non dimentichi il mio numero di telefono: otto sei cinque zero sei.	Don't forget my telephone number: 86506.
Centralinista, mi dia il numero quattro zero tre sei nove.	Operator, may I have 40369?
Il numero cinque sei otto sette cinque non risponde.	Number 56875 doesn't answer.

E. The Number is ...

Il numero è ...	The number is ...
Il mio numero è ...	My number is ...
Il numero della mia camera è trenta.	My room number is 30.
Io abito nella camera numero trenta.	I live in room 30.
Il numero della mia casa è mille trecento ventidue.	My address (house number) is 1322.
Io abito al numero trecento trentadue del viale Quinto, al quinto piano.	I live at 332 Fifth Avenue, fifth floor.

LESSON 19

A. What's Today?

Che giorno della settimana è oggi?	What's today? (What day of the week is today?)
È lunedì.	Monday.
È martedì.	It's Tuesday.
È mercoledì.	It's Wednesday.
È giovedì.	It's Thursday.
È venerdì.	It's Friday.
È sabato.	It's Saturday.
È domenica.	It's Sunday.

To say, "on Sunday ..." etc. in Italian, simply say the day:

Arrivo sabato.	I arrive (on) Saturday.
Vada lunedì.	Go (on) Monday.

To express a habitual action, use the definite article with the day of the week:

Non lavoriamo il sabato.	We don't work on Saturdays.
Mangio tardi la domenica.	I eat late on Sundays.

The following expressions all mean "What's the date?":

Quanti ne abbiamo?	(How many days do we have?)
A che data siamo oggi?	(At what date are we today?)
Che giorno è oggi?	(What day is today?)
Siamo al venti. **E il venti.** **Ne abbiamo venti.**	It's the 20th. (We're at the 20th.)

On + days of the month is expressed by the masculine definite article + a *cardinal number,* except for *first:*

il primo luglio	on July 1
il cinque aprile	on April 5

Che giorno è oggi?	What day is today?
È il primo maggio.	It's the 1st of May.
È l'undici aprile.	It's the 11th of April.
È il quattro luglio.	It's the 4th of July.
È il quindici settembre.	It's the 15th of September.
È il ventun giugno.	It's the 21st of June.
È il venticinque dicembre.	It's the 25th of December.
È il diciassette novembre.	It's the 17th of November.
È il tredici febbraio.	It's the 13th of February.
È il ventotto agosto.	It's the 28th of August.

B. Some Dates

L'America fu scoperta nel millequattrocento-novantadue.	America was discovered in 1492.
"I Promessi Sposi" furono pubblicati nel milleottocentoventicinque.	"I Promessi Sposi" ("The Betrothed") was published in 1825.

Dante nacque nel mille duecentosessantacinque, e morì nel milletrecentoventuno.	Dante was born in 1265, and died in 1321.
Noi siamo stati lì nel millenovecentoottanta quattro.	We were there in 1984.
Oggi è il ventidue febbraio millenovecentonovantadue.	Today is February 22, 1992.
Il suo compleanno è il quindici gennaio millenovecentocin–quantatre.	His birthday is January 15, 1953.
Nel diciannovesimo secolo ...	In the 19th century ...
Negli anni sessanta ...	In the Sixties ...

C. Word Study

conclusione	conclusion
cemento	concrete
contratto	contract
decisione	decision
persona	person
segnale	signal
stagione	season
stazione	station

QUIZ 17

1. *È lunedì.*	a. the 25th of June
2. *Che giorno del mese è oggi?*	b. the 28th of February
3. *il primo di luglio*	c. the 13th of August
4. *Che giorno è oggi?*	d. in 1990

5.	*l'undici aprile*	e.	It's Monday.
6.	*il ventotto febbraio*	f.	What day of the month is it?
7.	*il venticinque giugno*	g.	date
8.	*nel millenovecento novanta*	h.	the first of July
9.	*il tredici agosto*	i.	the 11th of April
10.	*data*	j.	What's the date?

ANSWERS

1—e; 2—f; 3—h; 4—j; 5—i; 6—b; 7—a; 8—d; 9—c; 10—g.

LESSON 20

A. What Time Is It?

Che ora è?	What time is it?
È l'una.	(It's) 1:00 o'clock.
Sono le due.	2:00.
Sono le tre.	3:00.
Sono le quattro.	4:00.
Sono le cinque.	5:00.
Sono le sei.	6:00.
Sono le sette.	7:00.
Sono le otto.	8:00.
Sono le nove.	9:00.
Sono le dieci.	10:00.
Sono le undici.	11:00.
Sono le dodici.	12:00 noon. It's noon.
È mezzogiorno.	12:00. It's noon.
È mezzanotte.	12:00 midnight. It's midnight.
minuto	minute

ora	hour
Che ora è, per favore?	What time is it, please?
Ha l'ora, per favore?	Do you have the time, please?
Il mio orologio fa le cinque.	It's 5 o'clock by my watch. (My watch marks 5 o'clock.)
È l'una e cinque.	1:05.
È l'una e dieci.	1:10.
È l'una e quindici.	1:15.
È l'una e un quarto.	1:15.
È l'una e mezza.	1:30.
È l'una e cinquanta.	1:50.
Sono le due meno dieci.	1:50 (two less ten minutes).
Sono le tre e dieci.	It's 3:10. (three and ten)
Sono le sei e tre quarti.	It's 6:45. (six and three quarters)
Sono le due meno un quarto.	It's 1:45. (two less a quarter)
Non sono ancora le quattro.	It's not four yet.
A che ora parte il treno?	At what time does the train leave?
Alle nove in punto.	At 9 o'clock sharp.
Alle nove precise.	Exactly at 9 o'clock.
Alle nove circa.	About 9 o'clock.
Verso le nove.	Around 9 o'clock.

B. At What Time?

A che ora?	At what time?
All'una.	At one o'clock.
Alle sette della mattina.	At 7 A.M.
Alle tre meno venti del pomeriggio.	At 2:40 P.M. (Twenty minutes to three).
Alle quindici meno venti.	At 2:40 P.M. (Fifteen hours less twenty minutes)
Alle sei di sera.	At 6 P.M.
Alle diciotto.	At 6 P.M.
Alle sei del pomeriggio.	At 6 P.M.

Notice that when you want to specify "A.M." or "P.M." in Italian, you add *di mattina* (of the morning), *del pomeriggio* (of the afternoon), *di sera,* (of the evening). In Italy, as in most European countries, the 24-hour system (used by the military in the U.S.) is generally used for transporation schedules and theatre times. From 1 A.M. to 12:00 noon, the time is the same as the 12-hour system. Afternoon, just keep counting, so that 1 P.M. is 13 hours, 2 p.m. is 14 hours, etc. Midnight, or 24 hours, is also expressed as 00:00.

C. It's Time

È ora.	It's time.
È ora di farlo.	It's time to do it.
È ora di partire.	It's time to leave.
È ora di andare a casa.	It's time to go home.
Ho molto tempo.	I have a lot of time.
Non ho tempo.	I don't have any time.
Lui sta perdendo tempo. Perde tempo.	He is wasting (losing) his time.
Lui viene di tanto in tanto.	He comes from time to time.

D. Word Study

assoluto	absolute
aspetto	aspect
bar	bar
cambio	exchange
certo	certain
combinazione	combination
maniera	manner
pericolo	danger
rischio	risk

QUIZ 18

1.	*È ora di farlo.*	a.	He comes from time to time.
2.	*Che ora è?*	b.	It's 9:00.
3.	*È l'una.*	c.	At what time?
4.	*Sono le tre.*	d.	It's time to do it.
5.	*Sono le nove.*	e.	It's 2:00
6.	*È mezzanotte.*	f.	It's 1:00.
7.	*A che ora?*	g.	I don't have any time.
8.	*Non ho tempo.*	h.	It's 2:40 P.M.
9.	*È l'una e un quarto.*	i.	It's noon.
10.	*Sono le quattro.*	j.	It's 3:00.
11.	*Sono le due.*	k.	It's 1:05.
12.	*Lui viene di tanto in tanto.*	l.	It's 4:00.
13.	*È mezzogiorno.*	m.	What time is it?
14.	*È l'una e cinque.*	n.	It's 1:15.
15.	*Sono le tre meno venti del pomeriggio.*	o.	It's midnight.

ANSWERS

1—d; 2—m; 3—f; 4—j; 5—b; 6—o; 7—c; 8—g; 9—n; 10—l; 11—e; 12—a; 13—i; 14—k; 15—h.

LESSON 21

A. YESTERDAY, TODAY, TOMORROW, ETC.

PASSATO	PRESENTE	FUTURO
ieri yesterday	**oggi** today	**domani** tomorrow
ieri mattina yesterday morning	**questa mattina (stamattina)** this morning	**domani mattina (domattina)** tomorrow morning
ieri sera last evening	**questa sera (stasera)** this evening	**domani sera** tomorrow evening
ieri notte last night	**questa notte (stanotte)** tonight	**domani notte** tomorrow night

B. MORNING, NOON, NIGHT, ETC.

questa mattina (stamattina)	this morning
ieri mattina	yesterday morning
domani mattina	tomorrow morning
questo pomeriggio	this afternoon
ieri pomeriggio	yesterday afternoon
domani pomeriggio	tomorrow afternoon
questa sera (stasera)	this evening
ieri sera	yesterday evening
domani sera	tomorrow evening
questa notte (stanotte)	tonight
ieri notte	last night
domani notte	tomorrow night

C. This Week, Next Month, in a Little While, etc.

questa settimana	this week
la settimana scorsa	last week
la settimana entrante	next week
la settimana prossima	next week
in due settimane	in two weeks
due settimane fa	two weeks ago
questo mese	this month
il mese scorso	last month
il mese entrante	next month
il mese che viene	the month that's coming
in due mesi	in two months
due mesi fa	two months ago
quest'anno	this year
l'anno scorso	last year
l'anno prossimo	next year
l'anno che viene	next year
in due anni	in two years
fra due anni	the year after next
due anni fa	two years ago
Quanto tempo fa?	How long ago?
un momento fa	a moment ago
molto tempo fa	a long time ago
ora	now, for the time being
in questo preciso momento	at this very moment
da un momento all'altro	at any moment
per il momento	for the time being
in questo momento	at this moment
in breve tempo	in a short time
in poco tempo	in a little while
di tanto in tanto	from time to time
Quante volte?	How many times?
una volta	once
ogni volta	each time
due volte	twice
raramente	rarely
non spesso	not often
molte volte **molto spesso**	very often

a volte **qualche volta**	sometimes
ogni tanto	once in a while
di tanto in tanto	now and then; from time to time
di mattina presto	early in the morning
al crepuscolo	in the evening (twilight)
al tramonto	at nightfall
il giorno seguente	the following day
il giorno dopo	the following day
fra due settimane	two weeks from today
fra una settimana	a week from today
domani a otto	tomorrow at eight
in una settimana	in a week
mercoledi prossimo	next Wednesday
il lunedì della settimana scorsa	Monday of last week
il cinque di questo mese	the fifth of this month
il cinque del mese passato	the fifth of last month
all'inizio di marzo	at the beginning of March
alla fine del mese	at the end of the month
all'inizio dell'anno	in the early part of the year
verso la fine dell'anno	toward the end of the year
Avvenne otto anni fa.	It happened eight years ago.

QUIZ 19

1. *ieri mattina*	a. last year
2. *questa sera*	b. last night
3. *domani sera*	c. today at noon
4. *ieri notte*	d. now
5. *l mese entrante*	e. in two weeks
6. *ora*	f. in a little while
7. *la settimana scorsa*	g. yesterday morning
8. *l'anno scorso*	h. from time to time

9. *oggi a mezzogiorno*	i. It happened eight years ago.
10. *in poco tempo*	j. this evening
11. *questa settimana*	k. sometimes
12. *Avvenne otto anni fa.*	l. within a week
13. *verso la fine dell'anno*	m. tomorrow evening
14. *due mesi fa*	n. next month
15. *verso la fine del mese*	o. last week
16. *in una settimana*	p. each time
17. *di tanto in tanto*	q. about the end of the month
18. *a volte*	r. toward the end of the year
19. *in due settimane*	s. this week
20. *ogni volta*	t. two months ago

ANSWERS

1—g; 2—j; 3—m; 4—b; 5—n; 6—d; 7—o; 8—a; 9—c; 10—f; 11—s; 12—i; 13—r; 14—t; 15—q; 16—l; 17—h; 18—k; 19—e; 20—p.

REVIEW QUIZ 4

1. *Compro un'automobile per* ________ (four thousand) *dollari.*
   a. *tremila*
   b. *quattrocento*
   c. *quattromila*
2. *Il numero del suo telefono è* ________ (40860).
   a. *sei, cinque, zero, sei, nove*
   b. *tre, sei, nove, due, zero*
   c. *quattro, zero, otto, sei, zero*

3. *Che* ________ (date) *abbiamo?*
   a. *giorno*
   b. *mese*
   c. *data*
4. *Che* ________ (day) *è oggi?*
   a. *mese*
   b. *giorno*
   c. *come*
5 .*il* ________ (17) *dicembre*
   a. *dicisassette*
   b. *ventisette*
   c. *cinque*
6. *È* ________ (1:10).
   a. *l'una e cinque*
   b. *l'una e dieci*
   c. *l'una e un quarto*
7. *Sono le* ________ (7).
   a. *sette*
   b. *nove*
   c. *sei*
8 .*È* ________ (12 noon).
   a. *mezzanotte*
   b. *mezzogiorno*
   c. *undici*
9. *Sono le* ________ (2:40).
   a. *le quattro meno un quarto*
   b. *le tre meno venti*
   c. *le due meno un quarto*
10. ________ (yesterday) *mattina*
   a. *oggi*
   b. *ieri*
   c. *e*
11. *la* ________ (week) *scorsa*
   a. *settimana*
   b. *notte*
   c. *domani*
12. *fra due* ________ (months)
   a. *settimana*
   b. *giorno*
   c. *mesi*

13. *Sono due* ________ (years).
   a. *mesi*
   b. *anni*
   c. *giorni*
14. *il* ________ (Wednesday) *della settimana entrante*
   a. *lunedì*
   b. *venerdì*
   c. *mercoledì*
15. *alla* ________ (end) *dell'anno*
   a. *fine*
   b. *inizio*
   c. *primo*

ANSWERS

1—c; 2—c; 3—c; 4—b; 5—a; 6—b; 7—a; 8—b; 9—b; 10—b; 11—a; 12—c; 13—b; 14—c; 15—a.

LESSON 22

A. Not, Nothing, Never, No One

The word for "not," *non,* comes before the verb:

io non vedo	I don't see
tu non vedi	you don't see
Non vedo nulla.	I see nothing. I don't see anything.
Non vado mai.	I never go.
Non vengono.	They are not coming.
Non vedo niente.	I see nothing. I don't see anything.
Non vado mai via.	I never go away.
Nessuno viene. (Non viene nessuno.)	No one is coming. (Nobody comes.)

Sì, signore.	Yes, sir.
No, signora.	No, ma'am.
Dice di sì.	He (She) says yes.
Dice di no.	He (She) says no.
Credo di sì.	I think so.
Non è bene.	It's not good.
Non è male.	It's not bad.
Non è quello.	It's not that.
Non è qui.	He's (She's) not here.
Non è troppo.	It's not too much.
Non è abbastanza.	It's not enough.
È abbastanza.	It's enough.
Non tanto in fretta. Non così in fretta.	Not so fast.
Non tanto spesso. Non così spesso.	Not so often.
Non è nulla. È nulla.	It's nothing.
Questo è nulla. Ciò è nulla.	That's nothing.
Non è molto importante.	It's not very important.
Non ho tempo.	I have no time.
Non so nè come nè quando.	I don't know how or when.
Non so dove.	I don't know where.
Non so nulla Non so niente.	I don't know anything.
Non ne so nulla. Non so nulla di ciò.	I know nothing about it.
Non voglio nulla. Non desidero nulla.	I don't want anything.
Non importa. Non fa niente.	It doesn't matter. It's not important.
Non me ne importa.	I don't care. It makes no difference to me.
Non me ne importa niente.	I don't care at all.
Non me ne importa affatto.	It doesn't make the slightest difference to me.
Non lo dica.	Don't say it.
Non ho nulla da dire.	I've nothing to say.
Non lo dirò mai.	I'll never say it.

Non è successo nulla.	Nothing happened.
Non ho niente da fare.	I have nothing to do.
Non lo vedo mai.	I never see him.
Non l'ho mai visto prima.	I've never seen him before.
Non l'ho mai visto.	I've never seen him.
Non viene mai.	He never comes.
Non è mai venuto.	He has never come.
Non vado mai.	I never go.
Non andrò mai.	I'll never go.

B. NEITHER ... NOR ...

Non ho detto una parola, nè una sillaba.
I haven't said a word, nor a syllable.

Non posso andare nè voglio andare.
I can't go, nor do I want to go.

Nè ... nè ...
Neither ... nor ...

Nè più nè meno.
Just so (neither more nor less).

Nè l'uno nè l'altro.
Neither the one nor the other. (Neither one.)

Nè questo nè quello.
Neither this nor that.

Nè molto nè poco.
Neither (too) much nor (too) little.

Nè bene nè male.
Just so-so. Neither good nor bad.

Non ho nè tempo nè denaro.
I have neither the time nor the money.

Non sa nè leggere nè scrivere.
He (she) can neither read nor write.

Non ho nè sigarette nè fiammiferi.
I have neither cigarettes nor matches.

C. Word Study

antagonista	enemy
avanzamento	advance
banco	bank
capitolo	chapter
contento	content
delizioso	delicious
energia	energy
errore	mistake
frutto	fruit
ricco	rich

QUIZ 20

1.	*Non vedo.*	a.	Neither this nor that.
2.	*Non è nulla.*	b.	I have no time.
3.	*Non lo dirò mai.*	c.	Don't tell it to me.
4.	*Non vado mai via.*	d.	Nothing happened.
5.	*Lui non vede Giovanni.*	e.	I don't see.
6.	*Non credo.*	f.	I don't know anything.
7.	*Non tanto in fretta.*	g.	I've never seen him.
8.	*Non so nulla.*	h.	He doesn't see John.
9.	*Non vedo nulla.*	i.	I'll never say it.
10.	*Io non l'ho mai visto.*	j.	He never comes.
11.	*Non me ne importa.*	k.	I see nothing.
12.	*Non è successo nulla.*	l.	I'll never go.

13. *Lui non viene mai.* — m. It's nothing.
14. *Non è male.* — n. He's not here.
15. *Non andrò mai.* — o. I don't think so.
16. *Non è qui.* — p. It's not bad.
17. *Nessuno viene.* — q. I don't care.
18. *Nè questo nè quello.* — r. Not so fast.
19. *Non me lo dica.* — s. I never go away.
20. *Non ho tempo.* — t. No one comes.

ANSWERS

1—e; 2—m; 3—i; 4—s; 5—h; 6—o; 7—r; 8—f; 9—k; 10—g; 11—q; 12—d; 13—j; 14—p; 15—l; 16—n; 17—t; 18—a; 19—c; 20—b.

LESSON 23

A. Isn't It? Aren't They? Don't You?

È vero?
Is it? (Is it true?)

Non è vero?
Isn't it? (Isn't it true?)

L'italiano è facile, non è vero?
Italian is easy, isn't it?

La gente qui è molto gentile, non è vero?
The people here are very nice, aren't they?

Lei non ha una matita, vero?
You don't have a pencil, do you?

Lei conosce questo posto, non è vero?
You know this place, don't you?

Lei conosce il signor Rossi, non è vero?
You know Mr. Rossi, don't you?

Lei ha un cucchiaio e un tovagliolo, non è vero?
You have a spoon and a napkin, haven't you?

Lei non è qui da molto tempo, non è vero?
You haven't been here very long, have you?

Lei verrà, non è vero?
You will come, won't you?

Fa freddo, non è vero?
It's cold, isn't it?

È molto carino! Non è carino?
Isn't it cute! It's cute, isn't it?

Va bene, non è vero?
It's all right, isn't it?

B. Some, Any, A Few

Ha (Lei) del denaro?
Do you have any money?

Sì, ne ho.
Yes, I have some.

No, non ne ho.
No, I don't have any.

Ha (lui) del denaro?
Does he have any money?

Ne ha.
He has some.

Non ne ha affatto.
He doesn't have any at all.

Ha ancora del denaro? Le è rismasto del denaro?
Do you still have money? Do you have any money left?

Me ne è rimasto un po'.
I have some left. (Some remains to me.)

Quanti libri ha?
How many books do you have?

Ne ho pochi.
I have few.

Desidera un po' di frutta?
Do you want some fruit?

Me ne dia un po'.
Give me some.

Ce ne dia un po'.
Give us some.

Ne dia un po' a lui.
Give him some.

alcuni dei miei amici
some of my friends

C. Like, As, How

come
like, as, how

come me
like me

come quello
like that

come questo
like this

come noi
like us

come gli altri
like the others

Questo non è come quello.
This one isn't like that one.

Ecco com' è.
That's how it is.

Come desidera.
As you wish.

È come a casa propria.
It's like (being at) home.

Lui non è come suo padre.
He's not like his father.

Non so come spiegare.
I don't know how to explain.

Com' è?
What's it like?

È bianco come la neve.
It's as white as snow.

Come piove!
What rain! (How it's raining!)

Come? Cosa dice?
What? What did you say? What do you mean?

Perchè no? Come no?
Why not?

QUIZ 21

1. *Come desidera.*	a. He's not like his father.
2. *come gli altri*	b. What? What did you say?
3. *come questo*	c. Give him some.
4. *Ha (Lei) del denaro?*	d. Why not?
5. *alcuni dei miei amici*	e. It's all right, isn't it?
6. *Non è come suo padre.*	f. As you wish.
7. *Come?*	g. Do you have any money?
8. *Ne dia un po' a lui.*	h. like the others
9. *Perchè no?*	i. like this
10. *Va bene, non è vero?*	j. some of my friends

ANSWERS

1—f; 2—h; 3—i; 4—g; 5—j; 6—a; 7—b; 8—c; 9—d; 10—e.

LESSON 24

A. Have You Two Met?

Buon di.
Hello. *(fam.)*

Salve.
Hi. *(fam.)*

Conosce il mio amico?
Do you know my friend? *(pol.)*

(È un) **piacere.**
(It's) a pleasure.

Credo che ci siamo già conosciuti.
I believe we've met before.

Non credo di aver avuto il piacere.
I don't believe I've had the pleasure.

Non ho avuto il piacere (di conoscerLa).
I haven't had the pleasure (of meeting you).

Credo che loro si conoscano già, non è vero?
I believe you already know each other, don't you?

Credo che ci conosciamo.
I think we know each other.

Ho già avuto il piacere di conoscerlo.
I've already had the pleasure of meeting him.

Mi permetta di presentarLa al mio amico Antonio Marchi.
Allow me to introduce you to my friend Antonio Marchi.

B. Hello, How are You?

Buon giorno.
Good morning. Good day.

Come sta?
How do you do? How are you getting along? *(pol.)*

Ciao.
Hi. *(fam.)*

Come stai?
How do you do? How are you getting along? *(fam.)*

Non c'è male. E Lei?
So, so. And you? *(pol.)*

E tu?
And you? *(fam.)*

E come sta Lei?
And how are you? *(pol.)*

E come stai tu?
And how are you? (*fam.*)

Che c'è di nuovo?
What's new?

Niente di nuovo.
Nothing much.

Nulla di importante.
Nothing much/important.

C'è niente di nuovo?
(Isn't there) anything new?

Non c'è niente di nuovo.
There's nothing new.

Com'è mai che non ci si vede?
Where have you been? *(fam.)*

Com'è che non La si vede mai?
Where have you been? (How is it that no one ever sees you?) *(pol.)*

Sono stato molto occupato in questi giorni.
I've been very busy these days.

Mi telefoni qualche volta.
Give me a call sometime.

Le telefonerò uno di questi giorni.
I'll call you one of these days. *(pol.)*

Ti telefonerò uno di questi giorni.
I'll call you one of these days. *(fam.)*

Perchè non viene a trovarci a casa?
Why don't you come to see us (to our house)?

Verrò a trovarvi la settimana prossima.
I'll come to visit you next week.

Non dimentichi la sua promessa.
Don't forget your promise. *(pol.)*

Non dimenticare la tua promessa.
Don't forget your promise. *(fam.)*

Alla prossima settimana, allora.
Until next week, then.

Arrivederci alla settimana prossima.
See you next week. (Until next week.) *(fam.)*

C. Word Study

angolo	angle
causa	cause
distanza	distance
effetto	effect
industria	industry
opinione	opinion
oscuro	obscure
proprietario	proprietor

LESSON 25

A. GLAD TO HAVE MET YOU.

Sono lieto di averLa conosciuta.
Glad to have met you.

Molto lieto (-a).
Glad (happy) to have met you.

Spero di vederLa presto.
Hope to see you again soon.

Lo spero anch'io.
I hope so, too.

Ecco il mio indirizzo e il mio numero di telefono.
Here's my address and telephone number.

Ha il mio indirizzo?
Do you have my address?

No, me lo dia.
No, let me have it.

Eccolo qui.
Here it is.

Molte grazie.
Thanks a lot.

Si sta facendo tardi.
It's getting late.

È ora di rientrare.
It's time to go back.

Partiamo domani.
We're leaving tomorrow.

Quando posso telefonarLe?
When can I call you?

Di mattina.
In the morning.

La chiamerò dopodomani.
I'll call you the day after tomorrow.

Aspetterò la sua chiamata.
I'll be expecting your call.

B. So Long

ArrivederLa.
So long *(pol.)*.

Arrivederci.
So long. *(fam.)*

Ciao.
Bye. *(fam.)*

ArrivederLa a presto.
See you soon.

A più tardi.
See you later.

A dopo.
See you later. *(fam.)*

Arrivederci ad un'altra volta.
So long, see you again. (Until another time.)

Alla prossima.
Until next time.

A domani.
See you tomorrow. (Till tomorrow.)

A sabato.
See you Saturday. (Till Saturday.)

Addio. Ti saluto.
Good-bye. (*fam.*)

QUIZ 22

1. *Spero di vederLa presto.*	a. Do you have my address?
2. *ArrivederLa.*	b. See you tomorrow.
3. *Sono lieto di aver la conosciuta.*	c. I'll be expecting your call.
4. *Ha il mio indirizzo?*	d. Till Saturday.
5. *Eccolo qui.*	e. In the morning.
6. *Di mattina.*	f. Glad to have met you.
7. *A domani.*	g. Thanks a lot.
8. *Aspetterò la sua chiamata.*	h. Hope to see you soon.
9. *Molte grazie.*	i. Here it is.
10. *A sabato.*	j. So long.

ANSWERS

1—h; 2—j; 3—f; 4—a; 5—i; 6—e; 7—b; 8—c; 9—g; 10—d.

C. Visiting Someone

Abita qui il signor Giovanni Rossi?
Does Mr. John Rossi live here?

Sì, abita qui.
Yes, he does. (He lives here.)

A che piano?
On what floor?

Terzo piano a sinistra.
Third floor on the left.

È in casa il signor Rossi?
Is Mr. Rossi at home?

No signore. È uscito.
No, sir. He's gone out.

A che ora sarà di ritorno?
A che ora ritornerà?
At what time will he be back?

Non so dirLe.
I can't tell you.

Desidera lasciar detto qualche cosa?
Do you want to leave him a message?

Gli lascerò un biglietto...
I'll leave him a note...

Se mi può dare una matita e un foglio di carta.
If you can give me a pencil and a piece of paper.

Ritornerò questa sera.
I'll come back tonight.

Ritornerò domani.
I'll come back tomorrow.

Ritornerò un altro giorno.
I'll come back another day.

Gli dica di telefonarmi, per favore.
Please tell him to call me.

Sarò in casa tutto il giorno.
I'll be at home all day.

QUIZ 23

1. *terzo piano a sinistra*	a. I'll be at home all day.
2. *Ritornerò più tardi.*	b. Is he at home?
3. *Abita qui il signor Giovanni Rossi?*	c. At what time will he be back?
4. *È uscito..*	d. He lives here.
5. *A che ora ritornerà.*	e. What floor?
6. *È in casa.*	f. Tell him to call me.
7. *Che piano?*	g. He's gone out.
8. *Gli dica di telefonarmi.*	h. Does Mr. John Rossi live here?
9. *Sarò in casa tutto il giorno.*	i. third floor on the left
10. *Abita qui.*	j. I'll come back later.

ANSWERS

1—i; 2—j; 3—h; 4—g; 5—c; 6—b; 7—e; 8—f; 9—a; 10—d.

LESSON 26

A. PLEASE

The most common ways of saying "please" are *per favore, per piacere,* or *mi faccia il favore,* which means literally "would you do me the favor of."

Mi faccia il favore di portare questo.
Please carry this.

Mi faccia il favore di venire.
Please come. (Do me the favor of coming.)

Ci faccia il favore di entrare.
Please come in. (Do us the favor of coming in.)

Facciano il favore di entrare.
Please come in. (speaking to several people).

Per favore, mi faccia vedere i suoi documenti.
Please let me see your papers.

Per piacere, vuol chiamare un tassì?
Will you please call a taxi?

B. OTHER POLITE EXPRESSIONS

1. **Abbia la bontà.**
   Please. (Have the goodness.)
   Abbia la bontà di dirmi dov'è la stazione.
   Can you tell me, please, where the station is?

2. **Mi scusi. Mi perdoni.**
   Excuse me. Pardon me.
   Scusi il ritardo.
   Excuse my lateness.

3. **Per cortesia.**
   Please.
   Per cortesia, il suo biglietto.
   Your ticket, please.
   Per cortesia, sieda qui.
   Please sit here.

4. **La prego.**
   Please. (I pray you.)
   La prego di farlo al più presto possibile.
   Please do it as soon as possible.
   La prego, puo dirmi dov'è la biblioteca?
   Can you please tell me where the library is?

5. **Mi dispiace. Mi spiące. Mi scusi.**
   I'm sorry.
   Scusami. Chiedo scusa.
   I apologize.
   Perdonami per favore. (per piacere, per cortesia)
   Please forgive me.

6. *Desidero,* or *desidererei,* means "I would like to."

Desidera sedere qui?	Would you like to sit here?
Desidererei andare ma non posso.	I'd like to go but I can't.

C. Word Study

ambizione	ambition
brillante	brilliant
capitale	capital
contratto	contract
democrazia	democracy
dipartimento	department
monumento	monument

ostacolo	obstacle
recente	recent

QUIZ 24

1. *Desidera sedere qui?*	a. Excuse my lateness.
2. *Per favore, venga qui.*	b. Excuse me. Pardon me.
3. *Per favore, vuol chiamare un tassì?*	c. Please come here.
4. *Scusi il mio ritardo.*	d. Please carry this.
5. *Mi scusi. Mi perdoni.*	e. Please tell me where the library is.
6. *Per favore, voglia entrare.*	f. Your ticket, please.
7. *Per favore, può dirmi dov'è la stazione?*	g. Will you please call a taxi?
8. *Per piacere, porti questo.*	h. Please come in.
9. *Per favore, il suo biglietto.*	i. Can you please tell me where the station is?
10. *Per favore, mi dica dov'è la biblioteca.*	j. Would you like to sit here?

ANSWERS

1—j; 2—c; 3—g; 4—a; 5—b; 6—h; 7—i; 8—d; 9—f; 10—e.

REVIEW QUIZ 5

1. *È in* ________ (home, house) *il signor Rossi?*
   a. *appartamento*
   b. *ora*
   c. *casa*

2. *Desidera lasciare un* ________ (note)?
   a. *matita*
   b. *biglietto*
   c. *carta*
3. *Abbia la* ________ *di dirmi dov'è la stazione.*
   a. *mi scusi*
   b. *bontà*
   c. *faccia*
4. *Mi facciano il* ________ *di entrare.*
   a. *bontà*
   b. *piacere*
   c. *servire*
5. ________ (Please) *lo faccia al più presto possibile.*
   a. *Servire*
   b. *Mi scusi*
   c. *Per piacere*
6. *Ha la faccia bianca* ________ (as) *la neve.*
   a. *cui*
   b. *come*
   c. *questo*
7. ________ (I would like), *ma non posso.*
   a. *Io desidererei*
   b. *Ho*
   c. *Desidera*
8. ________ (Why) *non lo ha detto?*
   a. *Chi*
   b. *Perchè*
   c. *Di chi*

ANSWERS

1—c; 2—b; 3—b; 4—b; 5—c; 6—b; 7—a; 8—b.

LESSON 27

A. WHO? WHAT? WHEN? ETC.

1. *Chi?* = Who?

Chi è?	Who is he (she)?
Non so chi è.	I don't know who he is.
Chi sono?	Who are they?
Chi lo ha detto?	Who said it?
Chi l' ha detto?	Who said so?
Chi l' ha fatto?	Who did it?
Di chi è questa matita?	Whose pencil is this?
Per chi è questo?	Who is this for?
Chi desidera vedere?	Whom do you wish to see?
A chi desidera parlare?	To whom do you wish to speak?
Chi lo sa?	Who knows it?
Di chi è questo?	Whose is this?

2. *Che? Che cosa?* = What?

Che cosa è questo?	What's this?
Che cosa è quello?	What's that?
Che cosa succede?	What's the matter? What's up?
Che c'è?	What's the matter? What's up?
Che è successo?	What happened?
Che c'è di nuovo?	What's new?
Cosa pensa? Che cosa pensa?	What do you think?
Cosa sono?	What are they?
Che cosa ha?	What do you have?
Cosa Le succede?	What's the matter with you?
Che ora è?	What time is it?
Che cosa dice?	What are you saying?
Che cosa ha detto?	What did you say?
Di che cosa sta parlando?	What are you talking about?
Di che si tratta?	What's it all about?
Che cosa vuole?	What do you want?

Cosa posso fare per Lei?	What can I do for you?
Desidera?	What do you want?
I signori desiderano?	What do you want? *(pol. pl.)*

3. *Perchè?* = Why?

Perchè così?	Why so?
Perchè no?	Why not?
Perchè dice questo?	Why do you say that?
Perchè tanta fretta?	Why are you in such a hurry? Why the hurry?
Perchè l' ha fatto?	Why did you do it?
Perchè non viene?	Why don't you come?

4. *Come?* = How?

Come si dice questo in italiano?	How do you say this in Italian?
Come si chiama?	What is your name? (How do you call yourself?) (*polite*)
Come ti chiami?	What is your name? *(fam.)*
Come si scrive questo?	How is this (written) spelled?

5. *Quanto?* = How much?

Quanto denaro desidera?	How much money do you want?
Quanti libri ci sono?	How many books are there?
Quanto è distante Napoli da Firenze?	How far is it from Naples to Florence?

6. *Quale?* = What? Which?

Qual'è il suo nome?	What is his name?
Quale desidera?	Which (one) do you want?
Quale desidera, questo o quello?	Which (one) do you want, this one or that one?
Quale di queste matite è la sua?	Which one of these pencils is yours?
Quale di queste due strade porta a Siena?	Which of these two roads leads to Siena?

Qual'è il Suo indirizzo?	What's his address? What's your address?

7. *Dove?* = Where?

Dov'è il Suo amico?	Where is your friend?
Dove vive (lui)?	Where does he live?
Dove và (lei)?	Where is she going?

8. *Quando?* = When?

Quando verrà Suo fratello?	When will your brother come?
Quando è successo?	When did that happen?
Quando parte?	When are you going (leaving)?
Non so quando.	I don't know when.
Fino a quando? Per quanto tempo?	Until when? For how long?
Non so fino a quando.	I don't know how long. (I don't know until when.)
Quando? Fra quanto tempo?	When?
Quando lei vuole.	When you wish.
Da quando?	Since when?
Com'è avvenuto?	How did it happen?
Quando è accaduto?	When did it happen?
Da quando è qui?	How long have you been here?

QUIZ 25

1. *Come si chiama?*	a. When did that happen?
2. *Quanti libri ci sono?*	b. Since when?
3. *Come si dice questo in italiano?*	c. Who knows?
4. *Che cosa dice?*	d. Where does he live?
5. *Quando è successo?*	e. What's your name?
6. *Da quando?*	f. What are you saying?
7. *Chi lo sa?*	g. Why not?

8. *Perchè no?* — h. How do you write that?

9. *Dove abita (lui)?* — i. How many books are there?

10. *Come si scrive questo?* — j. How do you say this in Italian?

ANSWERS

1—e; 2—i; 3—j; 4—f; 5—a; 6—b; 7—c; 8—g; 9—d; 10—h.

B. What a Pity! What a Surprise!

Che peccato!	What a pity!
Che vergogna!	What a shame!
Che disgrazia!	How Unfortunate! (What a misfortune!)
Che orrore!	How awful!
Che fortuna!	What Luck! How lucky!
Che sorpresa!	What a surprise!
Com'è carino!	How cute!
Com'è grazioso! Com'è bello!	How beautiful!

REVIEW QUIZ 6

1. *Non vedo* ________ (nothing).
   a. *nessuno*
   b. *nulla*
   c. *mai*
2. *Non viene* ________ (nobody).
   a. *nessuno*
   b. *no*
   c. *mai*
3. *Non sa leggere* ________ (nor) *scrivere.*
   a. *no*
   b. *mai*
   c. *nè*

4. *L'italiano è facile,* ________ (isn't it)?
   a. *non è vero*
   b. *è vero*
   c. *no*
5. *Me ne dia* ________ (a little).
   a. *nulla*
   b. *un po'*
   c. *qualcosa*
6. *Desidera* ________ (some) *di frutta?*
   a. *alcuni*
   b. *pochi*
   c. *un po'*
7. *Non è* ________ (like) *suo padre.*
   a. *come*
   b. *è*
   c. *gi altri*
8. *È stato molto* ________ (busy) *in questi giorni.*
   a. *sempre*
   b. *occupato*
   c. *nuovo*
9. *Si* ________ (know) *loro?*
   a. *conosciuti*
   b. *conoscono*
   c. *conoscerla*
10. *Con chi ho il piacere di* ________ (speak)?
    a. *parlare*
    b. *avere*
    c. *conoscere*
11. *Ecco il mio* ________ (address) *ed il mio numero di telefono.*
    a. *giorno*
    b. *biglietto*
    c. *indirizzo*
12. *Ci vedremo uno di questi* ________ (days).
    a. *giorni*
    b. *molto*
    c. *settimana*

13. *Lei ha la* ________ (mine).
   a. *molto*
   b. *mia*
   c. *giorno*
14. ________ (What) *dice?*
   a. *Come*
   b. *Quando*
   c. *Che*
15. ________ (Why) *è andata via?*
   a. *Che cosa*
   b. *Perchè*
   c. *Quanto*
16. ________ (How) *si dice questo in italiano?*
   a. *Come*
   b. *Quando*
   c. *Nessuno*
17. ________ (How much) *denaro desidera?*
   a. *A chi*
   b. *Quanto*
   c. *Di chi*
18. ________ (Who) *ha il suo vino?*
   a. *Chi*
   b. *Di chi*
   c. *Quale*
19. ________ (Where is) *il suo amico?*
   a. *Dov'è*
   b. *Come*
   c. *Chi*
20. ________ (When) *verrà suo fratello?*
   a. *Chi*
   b. *Quale*
   c. *Quando*

ANSWERS

1—b; 2—a; 3—c; 4—a; 5—b; 6—c; 7—a; 8—b; 9—b; 10—a; 11—c; 12—a; 13—b; 14—c; 15—b; 16—a; 17—b; 18—a; 19—a; 20—c.

LESSON 28

A. It's Good, It's Wonderful

Buono(-a).	Good.
È buono.	It's good.
Molto buono.	Very good.
È molto buono.	It's very good.
È eccellente.	It's excellent.
È stupendo.	It's wonderful.
È magnifico.	It's excellent. It's wonderful.
È ammirabile.	It's excellent. It's admirable.
È perfetto.	It's perfect.
È benissima.	It's great. (*fem.*)
È figo. È figa.	It's cool.
È di moda.	It's in (trendy).
È giusto.	It's all right.
Non c'è male.	It's not bad.
Va bene?	Is it all right?
Molto bene. Molto buono.	Very well. Very good.
È bella.	She's beautiful.
È bellissima.	She's very beautiful.
È molto carina.	She's very pretty, cute.
È attraente.	She's charming.
È bello	He's handsome.
È galante.	He's charming.
È carino.	He's cute.
È bravo.	He's a great guy.
È brava.	She's a good sport.
È molto alla mano.	She/He is a good sport.

B. It's Not Good, It's Worthless.

Non è buono(-a).	It's not good. It's no good.
Non è molto buono.	It's not very good.
Quello non è buono.	That's no good.
Questo non è giusto.	It's not right. This isn't right.

Questo non è corretto.	This isn't proper. This is wrong.
È male.	It's bad.
È molto male.	It's very bad.
È pessimo.	That's very bad. That's the worst.
È fatto malissimo.	It is done very badly.
È veramente cattivo.	It's really (truly) bad.
Non mi interessa.	I don't care for it. It doesn't interest me.
Questo non vale niente.	That's worthless.
Non serve a nulla.	It's worthless. It's good for nothing.
Uffa! Che noia!	It's a drag.
È orribile!	It's horrible.
È pessimo!	It's the worst.
Che schiffo!	It's digusting.

QUIZ 26

1. *Va bene.*	a. It's excellent.
2. *Molto bene.*	b. She's very pretty.
3. *È eccellente.*	c. That's worthless.
4. *Non c'è male.*	d. What a pity!
5. *È male.*	e. How unfortunate!
6. *Che peccato!*	f. It's wonderful!
7. *È molto carina.*	g. It's all right.
8. *Non serve a nulla.*	h. That's bad.
9. *Che disgrazia!*	i. Very well.
10. *È stupendo.*	j. It's not bad.

ANSWERS

1—g; 2—i; 3—a; 4—j; 5—h; 6—d; 7—b; 8—c; 9—e; 10—f.

LESSON 29

A. I LIKE IT.

Mi piace ...	I like ... (It pleases me ...)
Mi piace molto.	I like it (him, her) very much.
Mi piace moltissimo.	I like it (him, her) very much.
Mi piace quello.	I like that.
Lei mi piace.	I like her.
Mi piacciono molto.	I like them a lot.
La musica mi piace molto.	I love music.
Le piace?	Do you like it?
Non le piace?	Don't you like it?
Le piace la frutta?	Do you like fruit?
Si, la frutta mi piace.	Yes, I like fruit.
Non mi piace.	I don't like it.
Non mi piace molto.	I don't like it very much.
No, la frutta non mi piace.	No, I don't like fruit.
Le piace il cioccolato?	Do you like chocolate?
Le piace l'America?	Do you like America?
Le piace la cucina italiana?	Do you like Italian food?
Le piace l'Italia?	Do you like Italy?
Le è piaciuta l'Italia?	Did you like Italy?
L'Italia mi è piaciuta.	I liked Italy.
Crede che la casa piacerà loro?	Do you think they'll like the house?
Come piace Loro la mia camera?	How do you like my room? *(Speaking to several people.)*
Non mi piace.	I don't like it.
Non mi piace molto.	I don't like it very much.
Se Le piace.	If you like it.
Quando Le piace.	Whenever you like.
Quando desidera.	

Notice that the Italian for "I like fruit" is *Mi piace la frutta* (Fruit is pleasing to me). That is, the word which is the object in English is the subject in Italian. "I like the United States" is *Mi piacciono gli Stati Uniti* (The United States are pleasing to ne). Here the verb is plural because the subject *(gli Stati Uniti)* is plural.

B. I DON'T CARE.

Non m'importa.	I don't care.
Non me ne importa niente.	I couldn't care less.
Non me ne importa un fico secco.	I don't give a damn.
Non m'importa niente.	It doesn't matter.
Chi se ne importa?	Who cares?
Non importa *(niente).*	It doesn't make any difference.

C. I HAD A GOOD TIME.

Mi sono divertito(a).	I had a good time
Ci siamo divertiti un sacco!	We had a blast.
Non mi sono divertito(a).	I didn't have a good time.
È stata una perdita di tempo. È stato uno spreco di tempo.	It was a waste of time.
Divertiti! Buon divertimento!	Have a good time! *(singular)*
Divertitevi! Buon divertimento!	Have a good time! *(plural)*

QUIZ 27

1. *Le piace la cucina taliana?*	a. I don't like it very much.
2. *Le piace?*	b. Do you like my room?
3. *Mi piace molto.*	c. Do you like Italy?

4.	*Le piace la frutta?*	d.	If you like.
5.	*Quando le piace.*	e.	Don't you like it?
6.	*Le piace l'Italia?*	f.	I like it very much.
7.	*Non le piace?*	g.	Do you like it?
8.	*Se le piace.*	h.	Whenever you like
9.	*Non mi piace molto.*	i.	Do you like Italian food?
10.	*Le piace la mia camera?*	j.	Do you like fruit?

ANSWERS

1—i; 2—g; 3—f; 4—j; 5—h; 6—c; 7—e; 8—d; 9—a; 10—b.

LESSON 30

A. In, To, From, etc. (Prepositions)

Abito in Italia.	I live in Italy.
Sono stato a Roma.	I've been in Rome.
Vado a Roma.	I'm going to Rome.
Vengo da Roma.	I come (am) from Rome.
Parto per Roma.	I'm leaving for Rome.
Egli va verso Roma.	He's going towards Rome.
Sono andato fino a Roma.	I went as far as Rome.
Vado in Europa.	I am going to Europe.

1. *A* = To, In

a destra	to the right
a sinistra	to the left
due a due	two by two
poco a poco	little by little
a piedi	on foot

a mano	by hand
a mezzogiorno	at noon
a mezzanotte	at midnight
Si sono seduti a tavola.	They sat down at the table.
all' italiana	in the Italian manner
A domani.	Until tomorrow.
A presto.	See you soon. (Until soon.)
A più tardi.	See you later. (Until later.)
Arrivederci.	Good-bye.
Alla prossima volta.	Until we see each other again.

2. *Con* = With

Io sono andato con Giovanni.	I went with John.
Lui lo ha scritto con una matita.	He wrote it with a pencil.

3. *Di* = Of, From

È di mio fratello.	It's my brother's.
Io sono di Roma.	I am from Rome.
È fatto di legno.	It's made of wood.
di giorno	by day, in the daytime
di nuovo	again (of new)

4. *In* = In

Ho vissuto in Italia per vari anni.	I lived in Italy for several years.
Il treno partirà in orario.	The train will leave on time.
Venga in salotto.	Come into the parlor.
in quella direzione	in that direction.

5. *Fino a* = Up to, Until

fino a Milano	up to (as far as) Milano
Io sono salito fino al quinto piano.	I walked up to the fifth floor.

6. *Verso* = Toward, Around (Approximately)

Lei camminava verso il parco.	She was walking toward (in the direction of) the park.
Comincio a piovere verso mezzanotte.	It started to rain towards (around) midnight.

7. *Da* = From, Since

da Napoli a Capri	from Naples to Capri
da quando l'ho visto	since I saw him; since the time when I saw him

8. *Per* = For, Through, In place of

L'ho comprato per un dollaro.	I bought it for a dollar.
Gli ho dato un dollaro per questo.	I gave him a dollar for this.
Lui mi ha dato il suo libro per il mio.	He exchanged books with me. (He gave me his book for mine.)
Noi siamo passati per Roma.	We passed through Rome.
Il treno passa per Roma.	The train passes through Rome.
Lui entrò per la porta.	He came in through the door.
Io vado per lei.	I'll go for (in place of) you.
Io sarò in viaggio per due anni.	I'll be away traveling for two years.

9. *Sopra* = On, Above, Over

sopra la tavola	above the table
Lei aveva un capotto sopra le spalle.	She had a coat on her back.

10. *Su* = On, On top of

La tovaglia è sulla tavola.	The tablecloth is on the table.
Ha un velo sui capelli.	She has a veil on her hair.

B. Other Prepositional Expressions

a causa di	on account of
alla fine	finally at last
disposto a farlo	in favor of doing it
di conseguenza	consequently, as a result
di notte	at night
invece di questo	instead of this
in generale	in general
nella mattina	in the morning, during the morning
nel pomeriggio	during the afternoon, in the afternoon
Perchè?	Why? What is the reason?
per ora	for the time being
per esempio	for example
per quella ragione	for that reason
per ragione di	by reason of
Lui camminò per la strada.	He walked along the street.
Per amor di Dio!	For goodness' sake! For heaven's sake!
qui intorno	around here

C. Word Study

ballo	ball
biglietto	ticket
formaggio	cheese
civile	civil
educazione	education
efficiente	efficient
logico	logical
tavola	table

QUIZ 28

1.	*a mezzogiorno*	a.	on foot
2.	*poco a poco*	b.	one by one
3.	*a destra*	c.	I come from Rome.
4.	*all'italiana*	d.	It's made of wood.
5.	*con*	e.	by day
6.	*a piedi*	f.	again
7.	*Vengo da Roma.*	g.	on the table
8.	*È fatto di legno.*	h.	to the right
9.	*in rapporto a*	i.	in that direction
10.	*di nuovo*	j.	little by little
11.	*in quella direzione*	k.	until tomorrow
12.	*di giorno*	l.	at noon
13.	*a sinistra*	m.	since I saw him
14.	*uno a uno*	n.	in the Italian manner
15.	*fino a Milano*	o.	with
16.	*Partirò fra due giorni.*	p.	instead of
17.	*sulla tavola*	q.	to the left
18.	*a domani*	r.	in regard to
19.	*invece di*	s.	as far as Milano
20.	*da quando lo vidi*	t.	I'm leaving in two days.

ANSWERS

1—l; 2—j; 3—h; 4—n; 5—o; 6—a; 7—c; 8—d; 9—r; 10—f; 11—i; 12—e; 13—q; 14—b; 15—s; 16—t; 17—g; 18—k; 19—p; 20—m.

QUIZ 29

1. *per esempio*	a. I gave him a dollar for this.
2. *Il treno passa per Roma.*	b. I'll be away traveling for two years.
3. *Siamo passati per Roma.*	c. completely
4. *per ora*	d. for that reason
5. *L'ho comprato per un dollaro.*	e. around here
6. *per quella ragione*	f. For goodness' sake!
7. *Io sarò in viaggio per due anni.*	g. at last
8. *completamente*	h. for example
9. *Io gli ho dato un dollaro per questo.*	i. I am not in favor of
10. *Per amor di Dio!*	j. for the time being
11. *alla fine*	k. I bought it for a dollar.
12. *Lui entro per la porta.*	l. The train passes through Rome.
13. *qui intorno*	m. I take this instead of that.
14. *non sono disposto*	n. He came in through the door.
15. *Prendo questo invece di quello.*	o. We passed through Rome.

ANSWERS

1—h; 2—l; 3—o; 4—j; 5—k; 6—d; 7—b; 8—c; 9—a; 10—f; 11—g; 12—n; 13—e; 14—i; 15—m.

LESSON 31

A. On The Road

Scusi. Perdoni.
Excuse me. Pardon me.

Mi perdoni.
Pardon me.

Mi scusi.
Excuse me.

Qual'è il nome di questo paese?
What is the name of this town?

Quanto siamo distanti da Roma?
How far are we from Rome?

Quanti chilometri vi sono da qui a Roma?
How many kilometers from here to Rome?

È a dieci chilometri da qui.
It's ten kilometers from here.

È a venti chilometri da qui.
It's twenty kilometers from here.

Come arrivo a Roma da qui?
How do I get to Rome from here?

Segua questa strada.
Follow this road.

Come si arriva a questo posto?
How do you get to this place?

È molto lontano?
Is it very far?

Qual'è la via più breve per andare a Torino?
What's the shortest way to get to Torino?

Quale strada devo prendere?
Which road must I take?

Dov'è il parcheggio?
Where is the parking lot?

B. Walking Around

Può dirmi come posso arrivare a questo indirizzo?
Can you tell me how I can get to this address?

Può dirmi come posso arrivare a questo posto?
Can you tell me how I can get to this place?

Come si chiama questa strada?
What is the name of this street?

Puo indicarmi dov'è via Veneto?
Can you direct me to Veneto Street?

Dov'è questo indirizzo?
Where is this address?

È qui vicino via Barberini?
Is Barberini Street near here?

Penso di essermi smarrito (-a).
I think I'm lost.

Dov'è un telefono pubblico?
Where is there a public phone?

Può dirmi dov'è questa strada?
Can you tell me where this street is?

Dov'è via Rossini?
Where is Rossini Street?

È lontano da qui?
Is it far from here?

È vicino?
Is it near?

È la terza strada *(a destra).*
It's the third street on the right.

Vada per questa strada.
Go this way.

Vada avanti diritto.
Go straight ahead.

Vada fino all'angolo e volti a sinistra.
Go to the corner and turn left.

Prenda la prima strada a sinistra.
Take the first street to the left.

Volti a destra.
Turn right.

Dov'è la Questura?
Where is the Police Station?

Dov'è il Municipio?
Where is City Hall?

C. Taking a Bus, Train, Taxi or Subway

Dov'è la fermata dell'autobus?
Where is the bus stop?

A quale fermata scendo?
At what stop do I get off?

Si ferma qui l'autobus?
Does the bus stop here?

Dove scendo?
Where do I get off?

Dov'è la stazione ferroviaria?
Where is the railroad station?

Quanto è lontana da qui la stazione?
How far is the station from here?

Siamo ancora lontani dalla stazione?
Are we still far from the station?

Dove si prende il treno per Roma?
Where do you get the train for Rome?

Da quale binario parte il treno per Roma?
From which track does the train for Rome leave?

A quale binario arriva il treno di Roma?
At which track does the Rome train arrive?

Dov'è l'ufficio informazioni?
Where is the information office?

Vuole darmi per favore un orario ferroviario?
Will you please let me have a timetable?

Qual'è il treno per Roma?
Which is the train for Rome?

È questo il treno per Roma?
Is this the train for Rome?

Dove si prende il treno per Roma?
Where do you get the train for Rome?

Al binario due.
On track two.

Quando parte il treno per Roma?
When does the train for Rome leave?

Il treno è appena partito.
The train just left.

Il treno sta per partire.
The train is about to leave.

Quando parte il prossimo treno?
When does the next train leave?

Dov'è lo sportello dei biglietti?
Where is the ticket window?

Mi dia un biglietto di andata per Roma.
Give me a one-way ticket to Rome.

Di prima o di seconda classe?
First or second class?

Prima classe.
First class.

Quanto costa?
How much does it cost?

Cinquemila e cinquecento lire.
Five thousand and five hundred lire.

Quanto tempo ci vuole per arrivare?
How long does it take to get there?

Un po' più di un'ora.
A little more than an hour.

È occupato questo posto?
Is this seat taken?

Posso mettere la mia valigia qui?
May I put my suitcase here?

Che stazione è questa?
What station is this?

Quanto tempo ci fermiamo qui?
How long do we stop here?

Devo cambiare treno qui?
Do I change trains here?

Questo treno si ferma a Roma?
Does this train stop in Rome?

Tassì!
Taxi!

È libero?
Are you free (unoccupied)?

Mi porti a questo indirizzo.
Take me to this address.

Quanto Le devo?
How much do I owe you?

Si ferma qui il tram?
Does the streetcar stop here?

A che fermata devo scendere?
At what stop do I get off?

Dov'è la stazione della metropolitana più vicina?
Where is the nearest subway station?

QUIZ 30

1. *Qual'è la via più breve per andare a ...?*
2. *Dove posso telefonare?*
3. *Dov'è questa strada?*
4. *Mi porti a questo indirizzo.*
5. *Quanto è lontana la stazione?*
6. *Posso usare il suo telefono?*
7. *Può indicarmi dov'è via ...?*
8. *A che fermata devo scendere?*
9. *Come si arriva a questo posto?*
10. *Si ferma qui l'autobus?*

a. How far is the station?
b. How do you get to this place?
c. Can you direct me to ... Street?
d. Does the bus stop here?
e. At what stop do I get off?
f. Where can I phone?
g. Where is this street?
h. What's the shortest way to get to ...?
i. Take me to this address.
j. May I use your phone?

ANSWERS

1—h; 2—f; 3—g; 4—i; 5—a; 6—j; 7—c; 8—e; 9—b; 10—d.

LESSON 32

A. Writing and Mailing Letters

Vorrei scrivere una lettera.
I'd like to write a letter.

Mi può dare un po' di carta?
Could you let me have (give me) some paper?

Qui c'è carta e una penna.
Here is some paper and a pen.

Ha una matita?
Do you have a pencil?

Ha una penna?
Do you have a pen?

Ha un foglio di carta?
Do you have a piece of paper?

Ha una busta?
Do you have an envelope?

Ha un francobollo?
Do you have a stamp?

Dove posso comprare un francobollo?
Where can I buy a stamp?

Ha un francobollo aereo?
Do you have an airmail stamp?

Vado all'ufficio postale.
I'm going to the post office.

Dov'è l'ufficio postale?
Where is the post office?

Vorrei imbucare questa lettera.
I'd like to mail this letter.

Quanti francobolli occorrono per questa lettera?
How many stamps do I need on this letter?

Ho bisogno di un francobollo aereo.
I need an airmail stamp.

Ecco dei francobolli.
Here are some stamps.

Un francobollo espresso, per favore.
A special delivery stamp, please.

Dov'è la cassetta delle lettere?
Dov'è la buca delle lettere?
Where is the mailbox?

Dov'è la cassetta postale più vicina?
Where is the nearest mailbox?

All'angolo.
On the corner.

Dov'è la S.I.P?
Where is the public phone office?

È nell'ufficio postale.
It's in the post office.

B. Faxes and Telegrams

Devo spedire un facsìmile.
I have to send a fax.

Vorrei mandare un facsìmile.
I'd like to send a fax.

Quanto costa un facsìmile per Roma?
How much is a fax to Rome?

Da dove posso spedire un facsìmile?
From where can I fax?

Devo spedire un telegramma.
I have to send a telegram.

Vorrei mandare un telegramma.
I would like to send a telegram.

Quanto costa un telegramma per Roma?
How much is a telegram to Rome?

Quanto costa a parola?
How much is it per word?

C. TELEPHONING

C'è un telefono?
Is there a phone here?

Dove posso telefonare?
Where can I phone?

Dov'è il telefono?
Where is the telephone?

Dov'è la cabina telefonica?
Where is the phone booth?

Nell'atrio dell'albergo.
In the hotel lobby.

Posso usare il suo telefono?
May I use your phone?

Sicuro! Si accomodi!
Of course! Go ahead!

Posso fare una chiamata interurbana?
Can I make a long distance call?

Quanto costa una telefonata per Roma?
How much is a phone call to Rome?

Posso avere il numero otto, sette, cinque, otto, due?
May I have 87582?

Aspetti un momento.
Hold on a minute.

La linea è occupata.
The line is busy.

Centralino, Lei mi ha dato il numero sbagliato.
Operator, you gave me the wrong number

Non risponde.
There is no answer.

Posso parlare con il signor Ferri?
May I speak to Mr. Ferri?

In persona.
Speaking. (In person.)

Questo è il signor Villanova che parla.
This is Mr. Villanova speaking.

Parlo con il signor Ferri?
Am I speaking with Mr. Ferri?

Sono io.
Speaking.

Con chi parlo?
Who is this? (With whom am I speaking?)

Con il signor Ferri.
With Mr. Ferri.

QUIZ 31

1.	*Dove posso comprare un framcobollo?*	a.	Speaking
2.	*La linea è occupata.*	b.	May I have long distance?
3.	*Sono io.*	c.	On the corner.
4.	*Ha una busta?*	d.	There is no answer.
5.	*Posso fare una chiamata interurbana?*	e.	Where can I buy a stamp?
6.	*All'angolo.*	f.	the wrong number
7.	*Non risponde.*	g.	I'd like to send a fax.
8.	*Aspetti un momento.*	h.	Do you have an envelope?
9.	*il numero sbagliato*	i.	Hold on a minute.
10.	*Vorrei mandare un facìmile.*	j.	The line is busy.

ANSWERS

1—e; 2—j; 3—a; 4—h; 5—b; 6—c; 7—d; 8—i; 9—f; 10—g.

LESSON 33

A. What's Your Name

Come si chiama?
What's your name? *(pol.)*

Come ti chiami?
What's you name? *(fam.)*

Mi chiamo Giovanni Ferri.
My name is John Ferri.

Come si chiama?
What's her name?

Si chiama Maria Ferrari.
Her name is Maria Ferrari.

Come si chiamano?
What are their names?

Lui si chiama Giuseppe Riva e lei Anna Martini.
His name is Joseph Riva and her name is Anna Martini.

Qual'è il suo nome?
What's his (her) first name?

Il suo nome è Carlo.
His first name is Charles.

Qual'è il suo cognome?
What is his (her) last name?

Il suo cognome è Peretti.
His last name is Peretti.

B. Where Are You From?

Di dov'è Lei?
Where are you from? *(pol.)*

Di dove sei (*tu*)?
Where are you from? *(fam.)*

Io sono di Roma.
I'm from Rome.

Dov'è nato (nata)?
Where were you born?

Sono nato (nata) a Roma.
I was born in Rome.

C. How Old Are You?

Quanti anni ha?
How old are you?

Ho ventiquattro anni.
I'm twenty-four.

Compiro ventiquattro anni in settembre.
I'll be twenty-four in September.

Sono nato il diciannove agosto millenovecentosessanta.
I was born August 19, 1960.

Quando è il Suo compleanno?
When is your birthday?

Il mio compleanno è fra due settimane, il ventitrè gennaio.
My birthday is in two weeks, January 23.

D. Professions

Che mestiere fa?
What do you do?

Sono artista.
I'm an artist.

Che fa Suo padre?
What does your father do?

Che fa Sua madre?
What does your mother do?

È avvocato. (È avvocatessa.)
He's (she's) a lawyer.

È architetto.
He's (she's) an architect.

È insegnante.
He's (she's) a teacher.

È professore d'università. (È professoressa d'università.)
He's (she's) a university professor.

È dottore. (È dottoressa.)
He's (she's) a doctor.

È uomo d'affari.
He's a businessman.

È una donna d'affari.
(She's a businesswoman.)

È agricoltore. (È agricoltrica.)
He's (she's) a farmer.

È un funzionario dello Stato.
He's (she's) a government worker.

È operaio. (È operaia.)
He's (she's) a worker.

Lavora in una fabbrica di automobili.
He (she) works in an automobile factory.

E. Family Matters

Ha parenti qui?
Do you have any relatives here?

Quanti fratelli ha?
How many brothers do you have?

Ho due fratelli.
I have two brothers.

Il maggiore ha ventidue anni.
The older one is twenty-two.

Studia all'Università.
He is at the University.

Il minore ha quindici anni.
The younger one is fifteen.

Lui frequenta l'ultimo anno del ginnasio.
He's in his first year of high school.

Quante sorelle ha?
How many sisters do you have?

Ho una sorella.
I have one sister.

Ha nove anni.
She's nine.

Frequenta la scuola elementare.
She goes to grammar (elementary) school.

Vive qui tutta la Sua famiglia?
Does all your family live here?

Tutta la mia famiglia, meno i miei nonni.
All my family, except my grandparents.

Loro vivono in una tenuta vicino a Firenze.
They live in a country home near Florence.

È imparentato con il signor Villanova?
Are you related to Mr. Villanova?

È mio zio.
He's my uncle.

È mio cugino.
He's my cousin.

È imparentato con la signora Rossi?
Are you related to Mrs. Rossi?

È mia zia.
She's my aunt.

È mia cugina.
She's my cousin.

F. Word Study

ansioso	anxious
consolato	consulate
difficile	difficult
dottore	doctor
fine	end
futuro	future
lingua	language
terra	land

QUIZ 32

1.	*Ho una sorella.*	a.	What is his first name?
2.	*Di dov'è Lei?*	b.	I'm twenty-four.
3.	*Quanti anni ha?*	c.	Where are you from?
4.	*Qual'è il suo nome?*	d.	What are their names?
5.	*È mia zia.*	e.	She's my aunt.
6.	*È insegnante.*	f.	I have one sister.
7.	*Come si chiamano?*	g.	Are you related to Mr. Villanova.
8.	*Sono nato a Roma.*	h.	How old are you?
9.	*Ho venti quattro anni.*	i.	I was born in Rome.
10.	*È imparentato con il signor Villanova?*	j.	He's a teacher.

ANSWERS

1—f; 2—c; 3—h; 4—a; 5—e; 6—j; 7—d; 8—i; 9—b; 10—g.

LESSON 34

A. Shopping

1. **Quanto costa questo?**
   How much is this?

2. **Trentamila lire.**
   Thirty thousand lire.

3. **È piuttosto caro.**
   That's rather expensive.

   Non ha niente di più economico?
   Haven't you anything cheaper?

4. **Dello stesso modello?**
   Of the same style?

5. **Lo stesso modello o qualche cosa di simile.**
   The same sort or something similar.

6. **C'è questo.**
   There's this.

7. **Non ha nient'altro da farmi vedere?**
   Don't you have anything else you could show me?

8. **Meno caro?**
   Less expensive?

9. **Se è possibile.**
   If (it's) possible.

10. **Forse le piace questo?**
    Perhaps you like this?

11. **Dipende dal prezzo.**
That depends on the price.

12. **Questo costa diciassettemila lire.**
This one is seventeen thousand lire.

13. **Mi piace più dell'altro.**
I like it better than the other one.

14. **È più economico.**
It's cheaper.

15. **Com'è questo? È più economico o più caro?**
How about this? Is it cheaper or more expensive?

16. **È più caro.**
It's more expensive.

17. **Non ha altro assortimento?**
Haven't you anything else in stock?

18. **Spero di ricevere presto nuovi modelli.**
I'm hoping to receive some new styles soon.

19. **Fra quanto?**
How soon?

20. **Da un giorno all'altro.**
Any day now.

Puo ripassare verso la fine della settimana?
Can you drop in towards the end of the week?

21. **Lo farò ... Quanto costano questi?**
I'll do that ... What's the price of these?

22. **Tremila e cinquecento lire al paio.**
Three thousand five hundred lire a pair.

23. **Me ne dia una dozzina.**
Let me have a dozen.

24. **Vuole portarli con se?**
Will you take them with you? Will you take them yourself?

25. **Preferisco che me li mandi a casa.**
I'd rather have you send them to my house.

26. **L'indirizzo è sempre lo stesso?**
Is the address still the same?

27. **È lo stesso.**
It's the same.

28. **ArrivederLa.**
Good-bye.

NOTES

3. *È piuttosto caro* = That's rather expensive. *Molto caro* = very expensive. *Economico,* or *a buon mercato* = cheap. *Più economico* = cheaper. *Molto economico* = very cheap.

5. *Qualche cosa di simile* = something (of) similar.

7. *Da farmi vedere* = To make me see. You can also use *mostrarmi.*

19. *Fra quanto?* Idiomatic expression for "How soon?" It can also be expressed by *Fra quanto tempo?* (In how much time?)

20. *Da un giorno all'altro* = from one day to the other.

21. *Lo farò.* (I will do that.) Future of the verb *fare.*

23. *Me ne dia una dozzina.* (Give me a dozen "of them.") *Dia* is the imperative of *dare.*

24. *Con se* = with yourself.
Mandi: subjunctive of *mandare.*

28. *Arrivederla* is used instead of *arrivederci* because the speaker is addressing only one person.

QUIZ 33

1. *È abbstanza* ________ (expensive).
   a. *costa*
   b. *questo*
   c. *caro*
2. *Ha nulla di più* ________ (cheap)?
   a. *qualità*
   b. *prezzo*
   c. *economico*
3. *Della* ________ (same) *qualità.*
   a. *qualche cosa*
   b. *stessa*
   c. *più*
4. *Di* ________ (less) *prezzo.*
   a. *più*
   b. *meno*
   c. *stesso*
5. *Mi piace* ________ (more) *dell'altro.*
   a. *come*
   b. *più*
   c. *vale*
6. *Non* ________ (have) *maggiore assortimento?*
   a. *ha*
   b. *caro*
   c. *altro*
7. *Spero* ________ (receive) *notizie.*
   a. *scelta*
   b. *tranquillo*
   c. *ricevere*

8. *A* ________ (when)?
   a. *assortimento*
   b. *caro*
   c. *quando*
9. *Allo stesso* ________ (address)?
   a. *indirizzo*
   b. *domicilio*
   c. *spedire*

ANSWERS

1—c; 2—c; 3—b; 4—b; 5—b; 6—a; 7—c; 8—c; 9—a.

LESSON 35

A. Breakfast in a Restaurant

1. P[1]: **Hai appetito?**
   Are you hungry? (Do you have an appetite?)

2. Sig: **Sì, ho appetito.**
   I certainly am.

3. P: **Cameriere! Cameriere!**
   Waiter! Waiter!

4. C: **Cosa desidera?**
   What would you like?

5. P: **Vorremmo fare colazione.**
   We'd like to have breakfast.

6. Sig: **Cosa ci può servire?**
   What can you serve us?

[1] "P" represents Mr. Paoli. "Sig" stands for *Signora* (his wife), and "C" for *Cameriere* (Waiter).

7. C: **Caffelatte, tè con limone o con latte, cioccolata ...**
Coffee with milk, tea with lemon or with milk, hot chocolate ...

8. Sig: **Con che lo servite?**
What do you serve with it?

9. C: **Con panini, paste, biscotti ...**
Rolls, pastry, biscuits ...

10. Sig: **C'è del burro?**
Is there any butter?

11. C: **Sì signora.**
Yes, madam.

12. Sig: **Mi porti una tazza di caffè con latte.**
Bring me a cup of coffee with milk.

13. P: **Anche a me. E mi porti pure due uova fritte.**
The same for me. And bring me also two fried eggs.

14. Sig: **Cameriere, mi porta per favore un tovagliolo?**
Waiter, would you please bring me a napkin?

15. P: **Per me, una forchetta.**
And a fork for me.

16. Sig: **Per favore ci porti ancora un pò di zucchero.**
Please bring us a little more sugar.

17. P: **E poi ci porti il conto ... Ecco qui, cameriere ... tenga il resto.**
And then let's have a check ... Here you are, waiter ... keep the change.

18. C: **Molte grazie, signore.**
Thank you, sir.

NOTES

Breakfast is called *la prima colazione* to distinguish it from *la seconda colazione* (lunch). *Il pranzo* = dinner. *La cena* = supper.

1. The subject pronoun is not necessarily used when the meaning of the sentence is obvious.

2. *Ho appetito* = I have appetite.

4. *Che* is omitted. The sentence is really *Che cosa desidera?*

5. *Vorremmo,* condit. of *volere* (because it is a polite form).

9. *Panini* = rolls. *Panino imbottito* = sandwich (stuffed roll).

10. *Ha del burro?* = Have you some of the butter? *del (di il contraction) burro*

13. *Un uovo* = an egg. *Uova* = eggs. (Note the irregular plural.) *Uova con pancetta* = bacon and eggs. *Uova alla cocca* = soft-boiled eggs ("in the shell"). *Uova sode* = hard-boiled eggs. *Uova strapazzate* = scrambled eggs.

14. *Tenga:* imperative of *tenere* (polite form). *Il resto* = the rest, the change (as a tip). *Spiccioli* = change, small money.

QUIZ 34

1. ________ (We would like) *fare colazione.*
   a. *Vorremo*
   b. *Mangiare*
   c. *Appetito*
2. ________ (Is there) *del burro?*
   a. *Servire*
   b. *C'è*
   c. *Potrebbe?*

3. *Mi dia lo* ________ (same).
   a. *molto*
   b. *stesso*
   c. *spero*
4. *Chi va a* ________ (eat)?
   a. *servire*
   b. *poco*
   c. *mangiare*
5. *Io mangio molto* ________ (little).
   a. *vado*
   b. *questo*
   c. *poco*
6. *Per favore* ________ (bring me) *un tovagliolo.*
   a. *costume*
   b. *mi porti*
   c. *dirà*
7. ________ (Then) *ci porti il conto.*
   a. *Favore*
   b. *Forchetta*
   c. *Poi*

ANSWERS

1—a; 2—b; 3—b; 4—c; 5—c; 6—b; 7—c.

B. A Sample Menu

LISTA	MENU
Antipasto	Hors d'oeuvres
Minestrone	Vegetable soup
Passato di piselli	Pea soup
Frittata al prosciutto	Ham omelet
Pollo arrosto (pollo alla diavola)	Roast chicken (devil-style chicken)
Abbacchio (alla romana)	Roast lamb (Roman-style)
Bistecca con patate fritte	Steak with French-fried potatoes

Insalata verde con pomodori	Green (fresh) salad with tomatoes
Formaggio e frutta	Cheese and fruit
Caffè	Coffee

LESSON 36

A. APARTMENT HUNTING

1. **Sono venuta a vedere l'appartamento.**
I've come to see the apartment.

2. **Quale? Quale dei due?**
Which one? Which of the two?

3. **Quello che è da affittare.**
The one which is for rent.

4. **Ce ne sono due.**
There are two

5. **Me li può descrivere?**
Can you describe them?

6. **Quello al quinto piano non è ammobiliato.**
The one on the sixth floor is unfurnished.

7. **E quell'altro?**
And the other one?

8. **L'altro al secondo piano è ammobiliato.**
The one of the second floor is furnished.

9. **Quante camere ci sono?**
How many rooms are there?

10. **Quello al quinto piano è di quattro camere, cucina e bagno.**
The one on the fifth floor has four rooms, kitchen and bath.

11. **Dà sulla strada?**
Does it face the street?

12. **No, dà sul cortile.**
No, it faces the courtyard.

13. **E quello al secondo piano?**
And the one on the third floor?

14. **Quello al secondo piano ha una camera da letto, un salotto e una camera da pranzo.**
The one on the third floor has a bedroom, a living room, and a dining room.

15. **Dà anche sul cortile?**
Does it also face the court?

16. **No, dà sulla strada.**
No, it faces the street.

17. **Quanto è l'affitto?**
How much is the rent?

18. **Il più grande costa cinquecento mila lire al mese, più luce e gas.**
The larger one is 500,000 lire a month, plus light and gas.

19. **E quello ammobiliato?**
And the furnished one?

20. **Quello costa ottocento mila lire al mese, tutto incluso.**
That one costs 800,000 lire a month, everything included.

21. **Com'è ammobiliato? In che condizioni sono i mobili?**
How is it furnished? In what condition is the furniture?

22. **I mobili sono moderni e sono in ottime condizioni.**
It's modern furniture and it's in excellent condition.

23. **La biancheria e i piatti sono inclusi?**
Are linen and silverware (dishes) included?

24. **Troverà tutto quello che Le occorre, perfino una batteria da cucina completa.**
You'll find everything you need, even a complete set of kitchen utensils.

25. **Bisogna firmare un contratto lungo?**
Does one have to sign a long lease?

26. **Per questo dovrà vedere l'amministratore.**
You'll have to see the renting agent for that.

27. **Quali sono le condizioni?**
What are the terms?

28. **Un mese anticipato e uno di deposito.**
One month's rent in advance and another month's rent as a deposit.

29. **È tutto?**
Is that all?

30. **Naturalmente, dovrà produrre le Sue referenze.**
Of course you'll have to give references.

31. **A proposito, c'è l'ascensore?**
By the way, is there an elevator?

32. **No, non c'è ascensore.**
No, there isn't any elevator.

33. **Che peccato!**
That's too bad! (What a sin!)

34. **A parte questo, la casa è molto moderna.**
Aside from that, the house is very modern.

35. **Che cosa vuol dire?**
What do you mean?

36. **C'è l'aria condizionata centrale.**
There's central air conditioning.

37. **C'è una lavanderia?**
Are there any laundry facilities?

38. **Naturalmente. Le camere da bagno sono state rimodernate di recente.**
Of course. The bathrooms were recently remodeled.

39. **Si possono vedere gli appartamenti?**
Can one see the apartments?

40. **Soltanto la mattina.**
Only in the morning.

41. **Va bene. Verrò domani mattina. Molte grazie.**
Very well. I'll come tomorrow morning. Thanks a lot.

42. **Di nulla. S'immagini. Felice di poterLa servire.**
Not at all. Don't mention it. Glad to be able to help you.

NOTES

1. *A* = in order to.

4. *Ce* is used instead of *ci,* because *ci, mi, ti, vi,* become *ce, me, te, ve* before *ne.*

5. *Me li:* as in 4.

9. *Ci sono* = there are.

11. Idiomatic expression. *Dare* = to give, but also "to face."

13. The first floor in Italy is called *painterreno;* what we call the "second floor" in America is the *primo piano* in Italy.

21. *Il mobile* = piece of furniture. *I mobili* = the furniture *(pl.)*. *La mobilia, il mobilio* = furniture (*sing.*)

22. *Ottime:* superlative of *buone (fem. pl.)*.

23. *I piatti* includes dishes and silverware. *Il piatto da portata* = the serving dish. *L'argenteria* = the silverware.

26. *L'amministratore* = the manager.

30. Note article in front of *sue (possessive)*.

31. The definite article is often used in Italian where the indefinite is used in English.

33. *Che peccato!* = What a sin!

35. *Vuol:* the final *e (vuole)* of verb forms is often dropped in speaking.

38. *sono state rimodernate* = have been remodeled.

39. *Si possono vedere?* = Is it possible to see the apartments. (Impersonal use of verb: "Can one see ...")

42. *S'immagini* = imagine. A polite way to express "Don't mention it." Also: *Ma le pare.*

QUIZ 35

1. ________ (I've come) *per vedere l'appartamento.*
   a. *Sono venuta*
   b. *Sono*
   c. *Voglio*
2. *Quello* ________ (for) *affittare.*
   a. *in*
   b. *per*
   c. *da*
3. ________ (There are) *due.*
   a. *C'è*
   b. *Ce ne sono*
   c. *Sono*
4. *È* ________ (without) *mobili.*
   a. *con*
   b. *senza*
   c. *tra*
5. ________ (How much) *è l'affitto?*
   a. *Quando*
   b. *Quanto*
   c. *Troppo*
6. ________ (Does it face) *sulla strada?*
   a. *Guarda*
   b. *Faccia*
   c. *Dà*
7. *Dà* ________ (also) *sul giardino?*
   a. *altro*
   b. *anche*
   c. *poi*
8. ________ (It costs) *sei mila lire.*
   a. *Costa*
   b. *Quanto*
   c. *Vieneq*
9. *Bisogna* ________ (sign) *un contratto?*
   a. *scrivere*
   b. *segnare*
   c. *firmare*

10. *La casa è* ________ (very) *moderna.*
   a. *molto*
   b. *tanto*
   c. *male*

ANSWERS

1—a; 2—c; 3—b; 4—b; 5—b; 6—c; 7—b; 8—a; 9—c; 10—a.

B. To Have: *Avere*

io ho	I have
tu hai	you have
lui, lei ha	he, she has
noi abbiamo	we have
voi avete	you have
loro hanno	they have

a. It is also used in place of the english verb "to be" when talking about hunger, thirst, and other temporary conditions or feelings. *Avere* means "to have" in the sense of "to possess."

Io ho questo.	I have this. I've got this.
Io non ho nulla.	I don't have anything.
Lo ha lei?	Do you have it?
Io non l'ho.	I don't have it.
Io ho tempo.	I have time.
Io non ho denaro.	I haven't any money.
Io non ho tempo.	I haven't any time.
Lui non ha amici.	He hasn't any friends.
Io ho fame.	I'm hungry.
Io ho sete.	I'm thirsty.
Io ho sonno.	I'm sleepy.
Io ho freddo.	I'm cold.
Io ho caldo.	I'm warm.
Io ho ragione.	I'm right.

Lui non ha ragione.	He is not right.
Loro non hanno ragione.	They're wrong.
Ha (*Lei*) degli amici a Roma?	Do you have (any) friends in Rome?
Io non ho amici a Roma.	I don't have any friends in Rome.
Ha (*Lei*) una sigaretta?	Do you have a cigarette?
Io non ho sigarette.	I don't have any cigarettes.
Ha (*Lei*) un fiammifero?	Do you have a light (a match)?
Non ho fiammiferi.	I don't have any matches.
Io ho vent'anni.	I'm twenty.
(Io) ho mal di testa.	I have a headache.
(Io) ho mal di denti.	I have a toothache.
Che cosa hai?	What's the matter with you?
Non ho nulla.	Nothing's the matter with me.
Quanto denaro ha?	How much money do you have?
Io non ho denaro (affato).	I haven't any money (at all).
Io ho molto da fare.	I have a lot to do.

b. Do I have it?

L'ho *(Lo ho)* io?	Do I have it?
L'hai tu?	Do you have it? (*fam.*)
L'ha Lei?	Do you have it? (*polite*)
L'ha lui?	Does he have it?
L'abbiamo noi?	Do we have it?
L'avete voi?	Do you have it? (*fam. pl.*)
L'hanno loro?	Do they have it?
	Do you have it? (*polite pl.*)

c. Don't I have it?

Non l'ho *(Lo ho)* io?	Don't I have it?
Non l'hai tu?	Don't you have it? (*fam.*)
Non l'ha Lei?	Don't you have it? (*polite*)
Non l'ha lei?	Doesn't she have it?
Non l'abbiamo noi?	Don't we have it?
Non l' avete voi?	Don't you have it? (*fam. pl.*)
Non l'hanno loro?	Don't they have it?
	Don't you have it?(polite pl.)

QUIZ 36

1.	*Non ho denaro.*	a.	I have a headache.
2.	*Non ho nulla.*	b.	Don't you have it?
3.	*Lui non ha ragione.*	c.	I don't have it.
4.	*Ho sonno.*	d.	I'm cold.
5.	*L'ha lui?*	e.	I'm warm.
6.	*Non l'ho.*	f.	I don't have any money.
7.	*Ho fame.*	g.	Does he have it?
8.	*Ho freddo.*	h.	He's not right.
9.	*Ho venti'anni.*	i.	I'm thirsty.
10.	*Non l'ha lei?*	j.	I have a lot to do.
11.	*Io devo andare.*	k.	I don't have anything.
12.	*Ho caldo.*	l.	I'm sleepy.
13.	*Ho sete.*	m.	I'm hungry.
14.	*Ho mal di testa.*	n.	I have to go.
15.	*Ho molto da fare.*	o.	I'm twenty years old.

ANSWERS

1—f; 2—k; 3—h; 4—l; 5—g; 6—c; 7—m; 8—d; 9—o; 10—b; 11—n; 12—e; 13—i; 14—a; 15—j.

LESSON 37

A. Could You Give Me Some Information?

1. **Mi scusi.**
   Pardon me.

2. **In che cosa posso servirLa?**
   What can I do for you?

3. **Mi potrebbe dare alcune informazioni?**
   Could you give me some information?

4. **Con molto piacere.**
   Gladly. (With much pleasure.)

5. **Io non conosco questa città e non mi posso orientare.**
   I don't know this town and I can't find my way around.

6. **Bene, è abbastanza semplice.**
   Well, it's quite simple.

7. **Come vede, io sono straniera.**
   As you see, I'm a stranger (here).

8. **In questo caso Le mostrerò la città.**
   In that case I'll show you the town.

9. **La ringrazierò moltissimo. Lo apprezzerò molto.**
   I'd be very grateful to you. I'd appreciate that a lot.

10. **Vede quel gran palazzo all'angolo?**
    Do you see that large building on the corner?

11. **Quello con la bandiera?**
    The one with the flag?

12. **Esattamente. Quello è la Posta Centrale.**
    That's right. (Exactly.) That's the main Post Office.

Di fronte dall'altro lato della strada ...
Opposite, on the other side of the street ...

13. **Dove?**
Where?

14. **Da quella parte. Vede quell'altro palazzo con gli archi?**
Over there. Do you see that other building with arches?

15. **Oh, sì, adesso lo vedo.**
Oh, yes, now I see.

16. **Quella è la Galleria Colonna.**
That's the Colonna Gallery.

17. **La vedo. ... A proposito, qual'è il nome di questa piazza?**
I see it. ... By the way, what's the name of this square?

18. **Piazza San Silvestro.**
Saint Silvester Square.

19. **Dov'è la Questura?**
Where is the Police Station?

20. **In fondo a quella strada, a destra.**
At the end of the street, to the right.

21. **E se non la trovo?**
What if I miss it (if I don't find it)?

22. **Non si preoccupi.**
Don't worry.

È un gran palazzo grigio, con due guardie di fronte all'entrata.
It's a big, gray building with two guards in front of the entrance.

Vede quel negozio?
You see that store?

23. **Quale negozio? Quello a sinistra?**
Which store? The one on the left?

24. **Esattamente. Quello che ha quel grosso globo di vetro verde in vetrina.**
Right. The one with the large green globe (of glass) in the window.

25. **È una barbieria?**
It's a barbershop?

26. **No, è una farmacia.**
No, it's a pharmacy.

Al lato del negozio c'è la casa del dottore.
The doctor lives right next door. (Next to the store is the doctor's house.)

Il suo nome è sulla porta.
His name is on the door.

27. **Ha l'ufficio nella stessa casa in cui abita?**
Does he have his office there as well? (Does he have his office in the same house in which he lives?)

28. **Sì, ma tutte le mattine va all'ospedale.**
Yes, but he spends every morning at the hospital.

29. **Dov'è l'ospedale?**
Where is the hospital?

30. **Per raggiungere l'ospedale, Lei deve camminare per il corso Umberto, verso piazza del Popolo.**
To reach the hospital, you must take the Umberto Corso (Avenue), toward Popolo Square.

Alla penultima strada a sinistra si trova via San Giacomo, e l'Ospedale San Giacomo è là.
A block before reaching the Square, you will come to Saint Giacomo (James) Street, and there you'll find the Saint Giacomo hospital.

31. **Come posso ritornare al mio albergo?**
How can I get back to my hotel?

32. **Vada per questa strada. Lo vede là, dopo il ...**
Go this way. You see it there, next to the ...

33. **... cinema? Non è così?**
... movies? That's right, isn't it? (Isn't it so?)

34. **Esatto.**
Yes. (Exactly.)

35. **Ora ho capito.**
Now I understand.

36. **Perchè non si compra una guida?**
Why don't you buy yourself a guidebook?

37. **Non è una cattiva idea. Dove posso comprarla?**
That's not a bad idea. Where can I buy one?

38. **Alla stazione ferroviaria, oppure in qualsiasi edicola.**
At the station, or at any newspaper stand.

39. **È lontana da qui la stazione?**
Is the station far from here?

40. **La stazione si trova in piazza Cinquecento.**
The station is in Cinquecento (Five Hundred) Square.

41. **Dove si trova un edicola qui vicino?**
Where's there a newspaper stand near here?

42. **Ce n'è una all'angolo.**
There's one on the corner.

43. **La ringrazio molto.**
Thank you very much. (I thank you very much.)

44. **Non c'è di che.**
Not at all.

Sono molto lieto di esserLe stato utile.
I'm very glad to have been of help to you. (I'm very glad to have been useful to you.)

45. **Sono stata molto fortunata di averLa incontrata.**
I was certainly lucky to meet you.

Lei conosce questa città molto bene.
You really know this town very well.

46. **Non si sorprenda. Io sono il Sindaco.**
It's not surprising. (Don't be surprised.) I'm the mayor.

NOTES

2. *In che cosa posso servirla?* = In what thing can I serve you?

3. *Potrebbe:* conditional of *potere.*

5. *Orientarsi* = to orient oneself.

6. *Abbastanza* = enough.

9. *Apprezzerò:* future of *apprezzare.*

10. *Gran:* abbreviated form of *grande.*

12. *La posta centrale* = main post office. *La posta*= the mail.

14. *Palazzo* = building; also *edificio. Il palazzo* can also be "a palace."

24. In Italy, pharmacies usually have a green globe, or a big vase, in the window.

25. *La barbiera* = the barber shop; *un barbière* = a barber; can also be called *parrucchiere.*

30. *La penultima strada* = the street before the last. In Italy, people count by streets, not by blocks. There is actually no real word for block. *Caseggiato* is a group of buildings which might sometimes correspond to an American block.

33. *Cinema* is really the "Movie Theater." The movie (film) is called *la pellicola.*

35. *Ho capito* = I have understood. This is past tense, but this expression is often used instead of *capisco* with the same meaning.

37. *Cattiva* = bad, meaning literally "ugly." *Brutto* is also often used with the meaning of "bad." *Che brutta idea!* = What a bad idea!

44. *Non c'è di che.* (There is nothing abou it ... You are welcome.) A polite formula to use in answer to *grazie* (thank you). Another currently used expression is *prego.*
Sono molto lieto di esserle stato utile. (I am very glad to have been of help to you.) A polite expression.

46. *Non si sorprenda.* = Don't surprise yourself.

QUIZ 37

1. *È molto* ________ (simple).
   a. *poco*
   b. *semplice*
   c. *città*
2. *Le farò vedere la* ________ (city).
   a. *caso*
   b. *città*
   c. *orientare*

3. *Questo grande palazzo all'* ________ (corner).
   a. *angolo*
   b. *via*
   c. *ufficio postale*
4. *Questo è l'* ________ (post office).
   a. *via*
   b. *ufficio postale*
   c. *altro*
5. *Vede questo* ________ (store)?
   a. *destra*
   b. *negozio*
   c. *barbiere*
6. *Nella casa vicina c'è un* ________ (doctor).
   a. *dottore*
   b. *farmacia*
   c. *nome*
7. *Il suo nome è sulla* ________ (door).
   a. *stesso*
   b. *porta*
   c. *clinica*
8. *Ha l'ufficio nells stessa* ________ (house) *in cui vive?*
   a. *dopo*
   b. *lato*
   c. *casa*
9. *Un poco* ________ (before) *di arrivare alla strada principale.*
   a. *dopo*
   b. *prima*
   c. *passata*
10. *Dove posso* ________ (buy) *questo?*
    a. *comprare*
    b. *guida*
    c. *stazione*

ANSWERS

1—b; 2—b; 3—a; 4—b; 5—b; 6—a; 7—b; 8—c; 9—b; 10—a.

LESSON 38

A. Greeting an Old Friend

1. P: **Oh, eccoti qui! Come stai?**
Oh, there you are! How are you?

2. L: **E tu come stai?**
How are you?

3. P: **Non sei troppo stanco del tuo viaggio?**
Not too tired from your trip?

4. L: **Niente affatto!**
Not at all!

5. P: **Desidero presentarti a mia moglie.**
I'd like you to meet my wife.

6. L: **Con molto piacere.**
I'd be very happy to.

7. P: **Cara, ti presento Giovanni Lanzi.**
This is Giovanni Lanzi, dear.

8. L: **Molto felice di conoscerLa.**
I'm very happy to know you.

9. Sig: **Molto piacere.**
Glad to know you.

10. L: **E'stato un vero piacere per me di rivederti.**
It's been a real pleasure to see you again.

11. P: **Anche per me. Tu non sei cambiato affatto.**
I feel the same way about it. (For me, too.) You haven't changed a bit.

12. L: **E neanche tu.**
Neither have you.

13. Sig: **Cosa pensa la signora Lanzi degli Stati Uniti?**
How does Mrs. Lanzi like the United States?

14. L: **Le piacciono moltissimo.**
She likes it a lot.

15. Sig: **Deve essere molto diverso da Roma, no?**
It must be very different from Rome, isn't it?

16. L: **Negli Stati Uniti, decisamente, ci sono molte cose strane!**
There certainly are lots of very curious things in the United States.

17. Sig: **Per esempio?**
For example?

18. L: **Per esempio, non mi sarebbe mai venuto in mente di far colazione in una farmacia!**
For example, it certainly would never have come to my mind to have lunch in a pharmacy!

19. P: **Ma vuoi scherzare!**
You are joking!

20. L: **Niente affatto. Sto dicendo sul serio.**
Not at all. I'm very serious.

21. Sig: **Suvvia, ci racconti. Lei vuol dire che si può fare colazione ... in una farmacia?**
Come, tell us about it. You mean one can have lunch ... in a pharmacy?

22. L: **Certamente, signora. Lei può anche ordinare un bistecca.**
Naturally, madam. You can even have a steak.

23. P: **In una farmacia?**
In a pharmacy?

24. L: **Sì, in una farmacia, e con un ottimo gelato per dolce.**
Yes, in a pharmacy, and with excellent ice cream for dessert.

25. Sig: **Ma l'odore della farmacia, non disturba?**
But the smell of the pharmacy, doesn't that bother you?

26. L: **Non c'è nessun odore nelle nostre ...**
There isn't any smell in our ...

27. P: **Farmacie?**
Pharmacies?

28. L: **In America, non le chiamano farmacie, ma drug-stores.**
In America, they don't call them pharmacies, but drug-stores.

29. P: **Oh ... qui sta l'inganno! Le chiamano con nomi differenti!**
Oh ... that's the trick! They give them a different name!

30. Sig: **Ma come può questo cambiare le cose?**
But how does that change things?

31. P: **Allora, non è più una farmacia!**
Then it's no longer a pharmacy!

32. L: **Nel "drugstore" si vendono anche molte altre cose, come giocattoli, francobolli, sigarette, caramelle ...**
You also find other things in a drugstore: toys, stamps, cigarettes, candy ...

33. P: **Questo è veramente buffo!**
That's really very funny!

34. L: **... libri, carta da scrivere, utensili da cucina, articoli da toletta, e altro.**
... books, stationery, cooking utensils, toilet articles, and what-have-you.

35. P: **Allora, è un bazar?**
It's a bazaar, then?

36. L: **No, mio caro, è sempre un "drugstore!"**
No, my dear, it's (still) a drugstore!

NOTES

2. The *tu (fam.)* pronoun is used because two old friends are speaking.

4. *Niente affatto* = nothing done (*niente a-fatto:* from *fare*).

18. *Sarebbe venuto* = It would have come. (*Venuto:* past part. of *venire*. Double negation because the sentence begins with *non.*)

19. *Scherzare* = to joke. *Lo scherzo* = the joke. Other words are *la barzelletta, la freddura.*

20. *Sul serio* = on the serious side, or seriously.

21. *Suvvia* = Come on! The word is really composed of two expressions meaning "come on": *su* and *via.* Here the two words are linked by an extra *v.*

24. *Ottimo* is really the superlative of *buono,* meaning "excellent."

26. An example of the double negation often used in Italian.

29. *L'inganno* is also "deceit" from the verb *ingannare* (to deceive).

QUIZ 38

1. ________ (How) *stai?*
   a. *Qui*
   b. *Dove*
   c. *Come*
2. *Non sei troppo* ________ (tired) *dal tuo viaggio?*
   a. *affatto*
   b. *felice*
   c. stanco
3. *Desidero presentarti a mia* ________ (wife).
   a. *moglie*
   b. *molto*
   c. *piacere*
4. *È stato un vero* ________ (pleasure) *per me.*
   a. *cambiato*
   b. *piacere*
   c. *conoscere*
5. *Le piacciono* ________ (a lot).
   a. *moltissimo*
   b. *poco*
   c. *diverso*
6. *Ci sono molte* ________ (things) *strane!*
   a. *vero*
   b. *decisamente*
   c. *cose*
7. *Sto dicendo sul* ________ (serious).
   a. *serio*
   b. *scherzare*
   c. *venuto*
8. *Non le* ________ (call) *famarcie.*
   a. *chiamano*
   b. *inganno*
   c. *cambiare*
9. ________ (Then) *è un bazar?*
   a. *Allora*
   b. *Anche*
   c. *Sempre*

10. *Nel "drugstore" si vendono* ________ (stamps).
   a. *giocattoli*
   b. *francobolli*
   c. *caramelle*

ANSWERS

1—c; 2—c; 3—a; 4—b; 5—a; 6—c; 7—a; 8—a; 9—a; 10—b.

LESSON 39

A. Some Important Irregular Verbs

1. *Potere* = to be able

PRESENT	PRESENT PERFECT	FUTURE	PAST PARTICIPLE
io posso	**io ho potuto**	**io potrò**	**potuto**
tu puoi	**tu hai potuto**	**tu potrai**	
lui può	**lui ha potuto**	**lui potrà**	
lei può	**lei ha potuto**	**lei potrá**	
noi possiamo	**noi abbiamo potuto**	**noi potremo**	
voi potete	**voi avete potuto**	**voi potrete**	
Loro possono	**Loro hanno potuto**	**Loro potranno**	
loro possono	**loro hanno potuto**	**loro potranno**	

Posso?	May I? Can I?
Dove posso mandare un telegramma?	Where can I send a telegram?

Potrai venire questa sera? Will you be able to come tonight?

Posso parlare con lui? May I speak with him?

2. *Dovere* = to have to

PRESENT	PRESENT PERFECT	FUTURE	PAST PARTICIPLE
io devo	**io ho dovuto**	**io dovrò**	**dovuto**
tu devi	**tu hai dovuto**	**tu dovrai**	
lui deve	**lui ha dovuto**	**lui dovrà**	
noi dobbiamo	**noi abbiamo dovuto**	**noi dovremo**	
voi dovete	**voi avete dovuto**	**voi dovrete**	
loro devono	**loro hanno dovuto**	**loro devranno**	

Devo farlo. I must do it.
Io devo andare. I have to leave.
Io ti devo cinque dollari. I owe you five dollars.
Dovrei (conditional) **andarci.** I ought to go there.

3. *Volere* = to want

PRESENT	PRESENT PERFECT	FUTURE	PAST PARTICIPLE
io voglio	**io ho voluto**	**io vorrò**	**voluto**
tu vuoi	**tu hai voluto**	**tu vorrai**	
lui vuole	**lui ha voluto**	**lui vorrà**	
noi vogliamo	**noi abbiamo voluto**	**noi vorremo**	
voi volete	**voi avete voluto**	**voi vorrete**	
loro vogliono	**loro hanno voluto**	**loro vorranno**	

Voler bene a qualcuno. To like someone.
Voglio farlo. I want to do it.
Vorrei (conditional) **finire.** I would like to finish.

4. *Sapere* = to know

PRESENT	PRESENT PERFECT	FUTURE	PAST PARTICIPLE
io so	**io ho saputo**	**io saprò**	**saputo**
tu sai	**to hai saputo**	**tu saprai**	
lui sa	**lui ha saputo**	**lui saprà**	
noi sappiamo	**noi abbiamo saputo**	**noi sapremo**	
voi sapete	**voi avete saputo**	**voi saprete**	
loro sanno	**loro hanno saputo**	**loro sapranno**	

Lo so che è vero.	I know it's true.
Hai saputo la notizia?	Did you hear the news?
Essi lo sapranno in tempo.	They'll find out in time.

5. *Andare* = to go

PRESENT	PRESENT PERFECT	FUTURE	PAST PARTICIPLE
io vado	**io sono andato (-a)**	**io andrò**	**andato**
tu vai	**tu sei andato (-a)**	**tu andrai**	
lui va	**lui è andato**	**lui andrà**	
noi andiamo	**noi siamo andati (-e)**	**noi andremo**	
voi andate	**voi siete andati (-e)**	**voi andrete**	
loro vanno	**loro sono andati (-e)**	**loro andranno**	

Sono andato a piedi.	I walked. (I went on foot.)
Andremo insieme.	We'll go together.
Vada presto! (imperative)	Go quickly!
Adiamo!	Let's go!

6. *Venire* = to come

PRESENT	PRESENT PERFECT	FUTURE	PAST PARTICIPLE
io vengo	**io sono venuto (-a)**	**io verrò**	**venuto**
tu vieni	**tu sei venuto (-a)**	**tu verrai**	
lui viene	**lui è venuto**	**lui verrà**	
noi veniamo	**lei è venuta**	**noi verremo**	
voi venite	**noi siamo venuti (-e)**	**voi verrete**	
loro engono	**loro sono venuti (-e)**	**loro verranno**	

Vieni con me, non è vero?	You're coming with me, aren't you?
Viene sempre da me.	He always comes to my house.
Quando verrà Lei?	When will she come?
Vengono spesso in città.	They often come to the city.
Venga (imperative) **domani verso le tre.**	Come tomorrow at about three.

LESSON 40

A. FUN IN ITALIAN

UN'OTTIMISTA

Il capo di una importante casa commerciale, leggendo una richiesta di lavoro, si meraviglia moltissimo nel notare che il richiedente, pur non avendo esperienza, domanda uno stipendio eccessivo.

-Non le sembra di richiedere uno stipendio troppo alto, considerando la sua poca esperienza in merito?

-Tutt'altro, risponde il richiedente, assumere un lavoro del quale non si sa assolutamente nulla, è cosa molto più difficile, e dovrebbe essere pagata molto meglio.

AN OPTIMIST

The head of an important firm, looking at an application, is astonished when he notices that the applicant, though lacking experience, asks for a high salary.

"Doesn't it seem to you that you are asking for an excessive salary, considering the little experience you have?"

"On the contrary," replies the applicant. "Work performed by one who knows nothing about it is harder and should be better paid."

NOTES

1. *Si meraviglia moltissimo* = is very much amazed. *Meravigliarsi:* to wonder, to be astonished, to be surprised.

2. *Nel* is a contraction for *in il.*

3. *Pur* = although. (Always followed by the participle.)

4. *Non le sembra di richiedere?* = Does it not seem to you to ask? *Le sembra* = It seems to you. *Mi sembra* = It seems to me. *Ci sembra* = It seems to us.

5. *tutt'altro* = everything else, on the contrary.

6. *dovrebbe:* condit. of *dovere* (*dovrebbe* = it should be).

UNA PERDITA DI POCA IMPORTANZA

-Signora, per favore, mi dia una copia del "Messaggero." Non ho spiccioli. Può cambiarmi queste mille lire?
-Può pagarmi domani-risponde la giornalaia.
-E se morissi questa notte?
-Oh, non sarebbe davvero una grande perdita.

A MINOR LOSS

"Miss, please give me a copy of the *Messenger.* I don't have any change. Could you change this bill of one thousand lire for me?"
"You can pay for it tomorrow," says the woman selling the newspaper.
"What if I die tonight?"
"Oh, it wouldn't be a very great loss."

NOTES

1. *Spiccioli* = change, "little money."
2. *E se morissi:* if I die (past subjunctive of *morire*).
3. *Sarebbe:* conditional of "to be" (It would [not] be).

UNA LEZIONE DI ETICHETTA

Pietro e Giovanni vanno a mangiare in un ristorante. Entrambi ordinano una bistecca. Il cameriere li serve poco dopo. Pietro afferra subito la bistecca più grande. Giovanni, seccato, gli dice:
-Come sei maleducato! Ti servi per primo e ti prendi anche il pezzo più grande.
Pietro gli risponde:
-Se tu fossi stato al mio posto, quale pezzo avresti scelto?
-Il più piccolo, naturalmente.
-E allora, perchè ti lamenti? Non lo hai il più piccolo?

A LESSON IN ETIQUETTE

Peter and John go to a restaurant to eat. They both order steak. The waiter brings the steaks to them shortly afterwards. Peter grabs the larger steak. John says to him angrily:
"What bad manners you have! You helped yourself first and you took the larger piece."
Peter answers:
"If you had been in my place, which piece would you have taken?
"The smaller, of course."
"Then what are you complaining about? You have it, don't you?"

NOTES

1. *Entrambi* = both of them; also *tutti e due.*
2. *Sei:* familiar form of the present "to be." (Pietro and Giovanni are friends.)
3. *Se tu fossi stato* = if you had been. (The pluperfect subjunctive is used in this case to indicate a condition contrary to fact.)
4. *Avresti scelto:* past condit. of *scegliere;* expresses the second part of the condit. sentence. *Se io fossi stato in quel ristorante, avrei ordinato pollo arrosto.* If I had been in that restaurant, I would have ordered roast chicken.
5. *Lamenti* = you lament yourself. *Lamentarsi:* reflexive verb meaning "to lament," "to complain."

B. IMPORTANT SIGNS

Signori o Uomini	Men
Signore o Donne	Women
Gabinetto	Toilet
Chiuso	Closed
Aperto	Open
Proibito fumare	No Smoking
Vietato fumare	
Vietato l'ingresso	No Admittance
Bussare	Knock

Suonare il campanello	Ring
Strada privata	Private Street
Per informazioni rivolgersi qui	Inquire Within
Alt! Stop! Fermo!	Stop!
Via libera!	Go!
Attenzione!	Look out!
Pericolo	Danger
Rallentare	Go slow
Svolta obbligata	Detour
Attenzione	Caution (Look out)
Mantenere la destra	Keep to the right
Ponte	Bridge
Divieto di sosta	No Parking
Ufficio controllo	Check Room
Cambio	Money Exchange
Informazioni	Information
Sala d'aspetto	Waiting Room
Vietato sporgesi (dalla finestra)	Don't lean out (of the window)
Treno merci	Freight Car
Binario ferroviario	Railroad Track
Direttissimo	Express
Accelerato (locale)	Local
Fermata	Stop (bus, streetcar, etc.)
Vietata l'affissione	Post No Bills
In riparazione	Under Repair
Entrata	Entrance
Uscita	Exit
Camere ammobiliate	Furnished Rooms
Appartamenti	Apartments
Pittura fresca	Wet Paint
Incrocio	Crossroads
Macelleria	Butcher (Butcher's Shop)
Panificio	Bakery
Latteria	Dairy
Sartoria	Tailor Shop (also for women)
Calzoleria	Shoe store
Barbiere	Barbershop (barber)
Salumeria	Grocer

Farmacia	Pharmacy, Drugstore
Pasticceria	Candy Store
Cartoleria	Stationery Store
Cassetta delle lettere	Letter Box
Buca delle lettere	
Bar	Bar
Questura	Police Station
Vini	Wines
Distributore benzina	Gas Station
Libreria	Book Store
Commune municipo	City Hall
Bibite—Gelati	Drinks—Ice Cream
Acqua fredda	Cold water
Acqua calda	Hot water

QUIZ 39

1. *Entrata*	a. No Smoking
2. *Svolta obbligata*	b. Express
3. *Vietato sporgersi (dalla finestra)*	c. No Parking
4. *Chiuso*	d. Open
5. *Aperto*	e. Exit
6. *Vietato fumare*	f. Information
7. *Espresso*	g. Detour
8. *Divieto di sosta*	h. Entrance
9. *Uscita*	i. Closed
10. *Informazioni*	j. Don't lean out (of the window)

ANSWERS

1—h; 2—g; 3—j; 4—i; 5—d; 6—a; 7—b; 8—c; 9—e; 10—f.

FINAL QUIZ

1. ________ (Tell me) *dov'è la stazione.*
   a. *Mi permetta*
   b. *Mi dica*
   c. *Mi porti*
2. ________ (Can) *dirmi dov'è l'ufficio postale?*
   a. *Può*
   b. *Avere*
   c. *Costo*
3. Dove ________(is) *un buon ristorante?*
   a. *fare*
   b. *c'è*
   c. *oggi*
4. ________ (Bring me) *un po' di pane.*
   a. *Conoscer La*
   b. *Mi permetta*
   c. *Mi porti*
5. ________ (I need) *di sapone.*
   a. *Ho bisogno*
   b. *Avere*
   c. *Permette*
6. ________ (I would like) *un po' più di carne.*
   a. *Mi porti*
   b. *Mi manca*
   c. *Desidero*
7. *La* ________ (I introduce) *alla mia amica.*
   a. *presento*
   b. *ho*
   c. *venga*
8. *Dov'* ________ (is) *il libro?*
   a. *è*
   b. *quello*
   c. *questo*
9. *Abbia* ________ (the goodness) *di parlare lentamente.*
   a. *la bontà*
   b. *il piacere*
   c. *il favore*

10.________ (Do you understand) *l'italiano?*
  a. *Comprendo*
  b. *Parla*
  c. *Comprende*
11.________ (Go) *là.*
  a. *Vada*
  b. *Parla*
  c. *Essere*
12.________ (Come) *subito.*
  a. *Venga*
  b. *Vado*
  c. *Andiamo*
13.*Come si* ________ (call) *Lei?*
  a. *lavare*
  b. *chiama*
  c. *chiamano*
14.*Che giorno della* ________ (week) *è oggi?*
  a. *settimana*
  b. *mese*
  c. *anno*
15.*Che* ________ (time) *è?*
  a. *ora*
  b. *adesso*
  c. *ho*
16.*Non* ________ (I have) *sigarette.*
  a. *tempo*
  b. *ho*
  c. *avere*
17.________ (Do you want) *della frutta?*
  a. *Potrebbe*
  b. *Ha lei*
  c. *Desidera*
18.________ (Allow me) *di presentaLa al mio amico.*
  a. *Dare*
  b. *Mi permetta*
  c. *Mi porti*
19.________ (I want) *scrivere una lettera.*
  a. *Desidera*
  b. *Desidero*
  c. *Mi permetta*

20. *Quanto* ________ (costs) *un telegramma per Milano?*
   a. *costa*
   b. *costare*
   c. *conto*

21. *Desideriamo fare* ________ (breakfast).
   a. *colazione*
   b. *cena*
   c. *pranzo*

22. *È l'* ________ (1:45).
   a. *una a trenta*
   b. *una e quarantacinque*
   c. *una e quindici*

23. *Venga* ________ (tomorrow morning).
   a. *ieri mattina*
   b. *domani mattina*
   c. *domani a mezzogiorno*

24. *In che* ________ (can I) *servirla?*
   a. *può*
   b. *posso*
   c. *possono*

25. *Non* ________ (has) *importanza.*
   a. *avere*
   b. *ha*
   c. *avuto*

ANSWERS

1—b; 2—a; 3—b; 4—c; 5—a; 6—c; 7—a; 8—a; 9—a; 10—c; 11—a; 12—a; 13—b; 14—a; 15—a; 16—b; 17—c; 18—b; 19—b; 20—a; 21—a; 22—b; 23—b; 24—b; 25—b.

SUMMARY OF ITALIAN GRAMMAR

1. ALPHABET

LETTER	NAME	LETTER	NAME	LETTER	NAME
a	*a*	h	*acca*	q	*qu*
b	*bi*	i	*i*	r	*erre*
c	*ci*	l	*elle*	s	*esse*
d	*di*	m	*emme*	t	*ti*
e	*e*	n	*enne*	u	*u*
f	*effe*	o	*o*	v	*vu*
g	*gi*	p	*pi*	z	*zeta*

2. PRONUNCIATION

SIMPLE VOWELS

a	as in *ah* or *father*
e	as in *day, ace*
i	as in *machine, police*
o	as in *no, note*
u	as in *rule*

VOWEL COMBINATIONS

ai	ai in *aisle*
au	ou in *out*
ei	ay-ee
eu	ay-oo
ia	ya in *yard*
ie	ye in *yes*
io	yo in *yoke*
iu	you
oi	oy in *boy*
ua	wah
ue	way
ui	oo-ee
uo	oo-oh

CONSONANTS

h	is never pronounced
ll	When two consonants occur in
mm	the middle of a word they are both pronounced.
nn	Notice the difference between the following:
rr	*caro,* dear, *carro,* truck
ss	*casa,* house, *cassa,* case
	pala, shovel, *palla,* ball

SPECIAL ITALIAN SOUNDS

1. *ci, ce* is pronounced like the English *ch* in *chair:*

cacciatore hunter

2. *ch* before *e* and *i* is pronounced like the English *k* in *key*

chitarra guitar

3. *gh* before *e* and *i* is pronounced like the English *g* in *gate:*

ghirlanda garland

4. *gli.* The closest English approximation is the combination *lli* as in *million*

figlio son *paglia* straw

5. *gn* is always pronounced as one letter, somewhat like the English *ni* in *onion* or *ny* in *canyon:*

segno sign *Spagna* Spain

6. *sc* before *e* and *i* is pronounced like the English *sh* in *shoe:*

scendere (to) descend *sciroppo* syrup

7. *sc* before *a, o,* and *u* is pronounced like the English *sk* in *sky:*

scuola school *scarpa* shoe

3. STRESS

1. Words of two syllables are generally stressed on the first syllable, unless the other one bears an accent mark:

lapis	pencil	*città*	city
penna	pen	*virtù*	virtue
meta	goal	*metà*	half

2. Words of more than two syllables are generally stressed either on the syllable before the last, or on the syllable before that:

ancòra	more	*àncora*	anchor
dolòre	grief	*amòre*	love
scàtola	box	*automòbile*	car

4. USE OF THE DEFINITE ARTICLE

il and *lo* (masc. sing.)	*la* (fem. sing.)
i and *gli* (masc. pl.)	*le* (fem. pl.)

There are instances in which Italian uses a definite article where no article is used in English:

Il tempo è denaro.	Time is money.
La vita è piena di guai.	Life is full of troubles.
I lupi sono feroci.	Wolves are ferocious.
I cani sono fedeli.	Dogs are faithful.
L'oro è un metallo prezioso.	Gold is a precious metal.
Il ferro è duro.	Iron is hard.
Gli affari sono affari.	Business is business.
La necessità non conosce legge.	Necessity knows no law.

Remember that in Italian you generally find the definite article in front of a possessive adjective or pronoun:

Il mio libro è nero, il tuo rosso. My book is black, yours red.

But with relationship nouns in the singular, no article is used with the possessive adjective:

mio padre	my father
tuo fratello	your brother
nostro zio	our uncle

Only with *loro* (their or your), with *nonno, nonna* (grandfather and grandmother), and with *papà, mamma* (daddy, mama) is the definite article used with the possessive:

la loro mamma	their mother
il vostro nonno	your grandfather

In expressions like the following, Italian uses the definite article:

Tre volte la settimana	Three times a week.
Due dollari la libbra.	Two dollars a pound.

The definite article is used when talking about parts of the human body.

Il signore ha il naso lungo.	The gentleman has a long nose.

The definite article is always used with expressions of time:

Sono le due.	It is two o'clock.

With some geographical expressions:

L'Europa è un continente.	Europe is a continent.
Il Tevere è un fiume.	The Tiber is a river.

5. USE OF THE INDEFINITE ARTICLE

Un, uno, una

Italian uses no indefinite article in cases like the following ones:

Io sono maestro.	I am a teacher.
Che donna!	What a woman!
mezzo chilo	half a kilo
cento uomini	a hundred men

6. THE PLURAL

There is no special plural form for:

1. Nouns with a written accent on the last vowel:

la città	the city
le città	the cities
la virtù	the virtue
le virtù	the virtues

2. Nouns ending in the singular in *i,* and almost all the nouns in *ie:*

il brindisi	the toast
i brindisi	the toasts
la crisi	the crisis
le crisi	the crises
la superficie	the surface
le superficie	the surfaces

3. Nouns ending in a consonant:

il bar	the bar
i bar	the bars
il gas	the gas
i gas	the gases

7. THE PARTITIVE

1. The partitive is expressed in Italian in several ways:
   a. with the preposition *di* + a form of the definite article *il, lo, la:*

Io mangio del pane.	I eat some (of the) bread.
Io mangio della carne.	I eat some meat.
Io prendo dello zucchero.	I take some sugar.
Io leggo dei libri.	I read some books.
Io scrivo degli esercizi.	I write some exercises.
Io compro delle sedie.	I buy some chairs.

   b. by using *qualche* (only with singular nouns):

Io scrivo qualche lettera.	I write a few letters.
Io leggo qualche giornale.	I read a few (some) newspapers.

   c. by using *alcuni, alcune* (only in the plural):

Io ho alcuni amici.	I have a few friends.
Io scrivo alcune poesie.	I write a few poems.

   d. by using *un po' di:*

Io prendo un po' di zucchero.	I'll take some sugar.

2. In some cases, especially if the sentence is negative, Italian does not use any partitive at all:

Io non mangio cipolle.	I don't eat onions.

8. ADJECTIVES

1. Many adjectives end in *o* for the masculine:

SINGULAR

un caro amico	a dear friend (*masc.*)

In *a* for the feminine:

una cara amica	a dear friend (*fem.*)

PLURAL

In *i* for the masculine:

cari amici	dear friends (*masc.*)

In *e* for the feminine:

care amiche	dear friends (*fem.*)

2. Some adjectives end in *e* in the masculine and in the feminine:

un uomo gentile	a kind man
una donna gentile	a kind woman

In the plural these same adjectives end in *i,* in both the masculine and the feminine:

uomini gentili	kind men
donne gentili	kind women

9. Position of the Adjective

A qualifying adjective generally follows the noun if it adds something important to the noun; otherwise it precedes. Some qualifying adjectives, like adjectives of nationality or of color, almost always come after the noun:

la musica italiana	Italian music
il libro nero	the black book

Possessive adjectives, demonstrative adjectives, numerals, and indefinite adjectives generally precede the noun:

il mio amico	my friend
questo libro	this book
due penne	two pens
alcuni signori	a few men

10. Comparison

(così) ... come	as ... as
tanto ... quanto	as much as many ... as
più ... di or che	more ... than
meno ... di or che	fewer less ... than
Il mio appartamento è (così) grande come il tuo.	My apartment is as large as yours.
Ho tanto denaro quanto ne ho bisogno.	I have as much money as I need.
Hanno tanti amici quanto vogliano.	They have as many friends as they want.

After *più* and *meno,* either *di* or *che* can be used, but if the comparison is between two adjectives, or if there is a preposition, only *che* can be used:

Franco è più studioso di (or *che*) *Carlo.*	Frank is more studious than Charles.
Giacomo è più studioso che intelligente.	James is more studious than intelligent.
Ci sono meno fanciulli in campagna che in città.	There are fewer children in the country than in the city

Studia puì di quello che tu pensi.	He studies more than you think.

If the second term of the comparison is expressed by a pronoun, the object form is used:

Lui è più alto di me.	He is taller than I.
Io sono meno ricco di te.	I am less rich than you.
Lei è così coraggiosa che lui.	She is as brave as he.

SPECIAL USES OF THE COMPARATIVE

Some expressions with the comparative:

ancora del (dello, della, dei, etc.)	more
un po' più di	a little more
altro, -a, -i, -e	more
Voglio ancora del pane.	I want more bread.
Prendo un po' più di carne.	I take a little more meat.
Compriamo altri libri.	We buy more books.
Non più	no more (quanity)
non più	no longer (time)
Volete di più? No, non vogliamo di piu.	Do you want more? No, we don't want any more.
Lei non canta più.	She doesn't sing any more.
Tanto meglio!	Great! (So much the better.)
Tanto peggio!	Too bad! (So much the worst.)

11. RELATIVE SUPERLATIVE

The relative superlative (the most/the least/the ... -est) is formed by placing the appropriate definite article before *più* or *meno*. The second term, of/in, is translated with *di*, whether by itself or combined with the definite article:

Quest'uomo è il più ricco del mondo	This man is the richest in the world.

Lei e la piu famosa delle sorelle.	She is the most famous of the sisters.
Marco è il meno timido di tutti.	Marco is the least timid of all.

The subjunctive often follows the superlative:

È il quadro più bello che io abbia mai visto.	It's the most beautiful painting I have ever seen.

With the superlative of adverbs, the definite article is often ommitted, unless *possibile* is added to the adverb:

Parla più chiaramente di tutti.	She speaks the most clearly of all.
Parliamo il più chiaramente possibile.	We're speaking as clearly as possible.

12. Absolute Superlative

1. The absolute superlative is formed by dropping the last vowel of the adjective and adding *-issimo, -issima, -issimi, -issime:*

L'esercizio è facilissimo.	The exercise is very easy.

2. by putting the words *molto,* or *troppo,* or *assai* in front of the adjectives:

La poesia è molto bella.	The poem is very beautiful.

3. by using a second adjective of almost the same meaning, or by repeating the adjective:

La casa è piena zeppa di amici.	The house is full of (loaded with) friends.
La macchina è nuova nuova.	The car is brand new.

4. by using *stra-, arci-, sopra-, super-, extra-:*

Il signore è straricco. (or) *Il signore è arciricco.*	The gentleman is loaded with money.
Questa seta è sopraffina.	This silk is extra fine.

13. Irregular Comparatives and Superlatives

Some adjectives and adverbs have irregular comparatives and superlatives in addition to the regular forms.

ADJECTIVE	COMPARATIVE	SUPERLATIVE
good	better	the best
buono(a)	*piu buono(a)*	*il piu buono*
	migliore	*buonissimo(a)*
		otimo(a)
		il/la migliore
bad	worse	the worst
cattivo(a)	*peggiore*	*il/la peggiore*
	piu cattivo(a)	*il/la piu cattivo(a)*
		pessimo(a)
		cattivissimo(a)
big/great	bigger/greater	the biggest/greatest
grande	*maggiore*	*il/la maggiore*
	piu grande	*grandissimo(a)*
		il/la piu grande
		massimo(a)
small/little	smaller/lesser	the smallest
piccolo(a)	*minore*	*il/la minore*
	piu piccolo(a)	*il/la piu piccolo(a)*
		piccolissimo(a)
		minimo(a)

ADVERB	COMPARATIVE	SUPERLATIVE
well	better	the best
bene	*meglio(a)*	*il/la meglio(a)*
badly	worse	the worst
male	*peggio(a)*	*il/la peggio(a)*

14. Diminutives and Augmentatives

1. The endings *-ino, -ina, -ello, -ella, -etto, -etta, -uccio, -uccia* imply smallness:

cagnolino	puppy
gattino	kitty

2. The endings *-one, -ona, -otta* imply largeness:

omone	big man
stupidone	big fool

3. The endings *-ino, -uccio* indicate endearment:

tesoruccio	little treasure
caruccia	little darling

4. The endings *-accio, -accia, -astro, -astra, -azzo, -azza* indicate depreciation:

cagnaccio	ugly dog

15. Masculine and Feminine

Nouns referring to males are masculine; nouns referring to females are feminine:

il padre	the father	*la madre*	the mother

il figlio	the son	*la figlia*	the daughter
l'uomo	the man	*la donna*	the woman
il toro	the bull	*la vacca*	the cow
il gatto	the tomcat	*la gatta*	the female cat

MASCULINE NOUNS

1. Nouns ending in *-o* are usually masculine:

il corpo	the body
il cielo	the sky
il denaro	the money

2. The names of the months and the names of the days (except Sunday) are masculine:

il gennaio	January
il lunedì	Monday

3. The names of lakes and many names of mountains are masculine:

il Garda	Lake Garda
gli Appennini	the Appenines

FEMININE NOUNS

Nouns ending in *-a* are usually feminine:

la testa	the head
la città	the city
la quantità	the quantity

Nouns ending in *-e*

Nouns ending in *-e* in the singular may be either masculine or feminine:

la madre	the mother

il padre	the father
la legge	the law
il piede	the foot

NOUNS WITH MASCULINE AND FEMININE FORMS

1. Some masculine nouns ending in *-a, -e, -o* form their feminine in *-essa:*

il poeta	the poet	*la poetessa*	he poetess
il conte	the count	*la contessa*	the countess

2. Masculine nouns ending in *-tore* form their feminine in *-trice:*

l'attore	the actor	*l'attrice*	the actress

16. Plural of Nouns

1. Nouns ending in *-o,* mostly masculine, form their plural in *-i:*

il lupo	the wolf	*i lupi*	the wolves

SOME EXCEPTIONS

Some nouns ending in *-o* are, feminine:

la mano	the hand	*le mani*	the hands
la radio	the radio	*le radio*	the radios
la dinamo	the dynamo	*le dinamo*	the dynamos

Some masculine nouns ending in *-o* have two plurals with different meanings for each plural:

il braccio	the arm
i bracci	the arms (of a stream)
le braccia	the arms (of the body)

2. Nouns ending in *-a,* usually feminine, form their plural in *-e:*

la rosa	the rose	*le rose*	the roses

A number of masculine nouns ending in *-a* form their plural in *-i:*

il poeta	the poet	*i poeti*	the poets

3. Nouns ending in *-e,* which can be masculine or feminine, form their plural in *-i:*

il nipote	the nephew or grandson	*i nipoti*	the nephews or grandsons
la nipote	the niece or granddaughter	*le nipoti*	the nieces or granddaughters

SPECIAL CASES

1. Nouns ending in *-ca* or *-ga* insert *h* in the plural:

la barca	the boat	*le barche*	the boats
il monarca	the monarch	*i monarchi*	the monarchs

Exception:

un Belga	a Belgian	*i Belgi*	the Belgians

2. Nouns ending in *-cia* or *-gia* (with unaccented *i*) form their plural in *-ce* or *-ge* if the *c* or *g* are double or preceded by another consonant:

la spiaggia	the seashore	*le spiagge*	the seashores
la guancia	the cheek	*le guance*	the cheeks

Nouns ending in *-cia* or *-gia* form their plural in *-cie* or*-gie* if *c* or *g* is preceded by a vowel or if the *i* is accented:

la fiducia	the trust	*le fiducie*	the trusts
le bugia	the lie	*le bugie*	the lies

3. Nouns ending in *-io* (without an accent on the *i*) have a single *i* in the plural:

il figlio	the son	*i figli*	the sons

If the *i* is accented, the plural has *ii:*

lo zio	the uncle	*gli zii*	the uncles

4. Nouns ending in *-co* or *-go* form their plural in *-chi* or *-ghi,* if the accent falls on the syllable before the last:

il fico	the fig	*i fichi*	the figs

Exception:

l'amico	the friend	*gli amici*	the friends

If the accent falls on the second syllable before the last, the plural is in *-ci* or *-gi:*

il medico	the doctor	*i medici*	the doctors

5. Nouns in the singular with the accent on the last vowel do not change in the plural:

la città	the city	*le città*	the cities

17. Days of the Week

The days of the week (except Sunday) are masculine and are not capitalized. The article is unnecessary unless "on Sundays" "on Mondays," etc. is meant.

lunedì	Monday
martedì	Tuesday
mercoledì	Wednesday
giovedì	Thursday
venerdì	Friday
sabato	Saturday
domenica (fem.)	Sunday

Domenica è il primo giorno della settimana.	Sunday is the first day of the week.
Andranno a far loro visita domenica.	They're going to pay them a visit on Sunday.
Domani è sabato.	Tomorrow is Saturday.
La domenica vado in chiesa.	On Sundays I go to church.
Vado a scuola il venerdì.	I go to school on Fridays.

Note: The word *on* is not translated before the days of the week or a date.

il 15 febbraio	on February 15

18. Months of the Year

The names of the months are masculine and are not capitalized. They are usually used without the definite article:

gennaio	January
febbraio	February
marzo	March
aprile	April
maggio	May
giugno	June
luglio	July
agosto	August
settembre	September
ottobre	October
novembre	November
dicembre	December

19. The Seasons

l'inverno (masc.)	winter
la primavera	spring
l'estate (fem.)	summer
l'autunno (masc.)	fall

The names of the seasons are usually not capitalized. They are preceded by the definite article, but after *di* the article may or may not be used:

L'inverno è una brutta stagione.	Winter is an ugly season.
Fa freddo d'inverno.	It's cold in (the) winter.
Io lavoro durante i mesi d'estate (or dell'estate).	I work during the summer months.

20. Numbers

The plural of *mille* (thousand) is *mila; duemila,* two thousand; *seimila,* six thousand.

After *milione* the preposition *di* is used:

un milione di soldati	one million soldiers
tre milioni di dollari	three million dollars

In writing a date, give the day first and then the month:

5 (cinque) agosto	August 5th
10 (dieci) novembre	November 10th

Only for the first of the month is the ordinal numeral used:

il primo novembre	November 1st
il tre agosto	August 3rd

21. Demonstratives

questo, -a, -i, -e	this, these
quello, -a, -i, -e	that, those

The pronoun "this" is *questo:*

Questo è l'uomo che cerchiamo.	This is the man we are looking for.

Besides the forms of *quello* already given, there are also the forms *quel, quei, quegli.* Here is how they are used:

1. If the article *il* is used before the noun, use *quel:*

il libro	the book
quel libro	that book

2. If *i* is used before the noun, use *quei:*

i maestri	the teachers
quei maestri	those teachers

3. If *gli* is used before the noun, use *quegli:*

gli studenti	the students
quegli studenti	those students

The same forms and the same rules apply to *bel, bei, begli,* from *bello, -a,-i, -e,* beautiful.

22. Possessive Adjectives

Always use the article in front of a possessive adjective:

il mio denaro	my money
la tua sedia	your chair
la vostra borsa	your pocketbook

Except for members of the family in the singular:

mia madre	my mother

The possessive adjective agrees with the thing possessed and not with the possessor:

la sua chiave	(his, her) key

Suo may mean *his* or *her* or, with the polite form, *your.* If confusion should arise by using *suo,* use *di lui, di lei,* etc.

23. Indefinite Adjectives

1. *qualche* (used only in *sing.*) some
   alcuni (used only in the *pl.*) some

qualche lettera	some letters
alcuni dollari	some dollars

Note: *Alcuni* can be also used as a pronoun: *alcuni ... altri* (some ... others).

2. *qualunque, qualsiasi* (has no *pl.*) any

qualunque mese	any month
qualsiasi ragazzo	any boy

3. *ogni* (has no *pl.*)	every or each
ciascun ciascuno ciascuna (no pl.)	each or every
Ogni ragazzo parla.	Every boy talks.
Ogni ragazza parla.	Every girl talks.
Diciamo una parola a ciascun signore.	Let's say a word to each gentlemen.
Raccontate tutto a ciascuna signora.	Tell everything to each (or every) lady
4. *altro (l'altro), altra, altri, altre*	other or more
Mandiamo gli altri libri?	Do we send the other books?
Vuole altro denaro?	Do you want more money?
5. *nessuno, nessun, nessuna*	no, no one
Nessuno zio ha scritto.	No uncle wrote.
Nessun soldato ha paura.	No soldier is afraid.
Nessuna sedia è buona.	No chair is good.

24. Indefinite Pronouns

1. *alcuni*	some
alcuni ... altri	some ... some
alcuni dei suoi discorsi	some of his speeches
Di questi libri a alcuni sono buoni, altri cattivi.	Of these books some are good, some bad.
2. *qualcuno, qualcheduno (no fem. no pl.)*	someone somebody
Qualcuno è venuto.	Somebody came.
Qualcheduno ci chiama	Somebody is calling us.
3. *chiunque, chicchessia (no fem., no pl.)*	anybody, any one

Chiunque dice così	Anybody says so.

4. *ognuno* (only *sing.*), *tutti* (only *pl.*)	everybody, everyone
ciascuno (only *sing.*), *tutto*	each or each one, everything
Ognuno corre.	Everybody runs.
Tutti corrono.	Everybody runs. (All run.)

5. *l'altro, l'altra, gli altri, le altre, altro*	the other, the others. in interrogative or negative sentences) else, anything else
un altro	another one
Lui dice una cosa ma l'altro non è d'accordo.	He says one thing but the other one does not agree.
Volete altro?	Do you want something else?
Non vogliamo altro.	We do not want anything else.

6. *niente, nulla*	nothing
nessuno (no *fem.*, no *pl.*)	nobody, no one
Niente (nulla) lo consola.	Nothing consoles him.
Nessuno conosce questa regola.	Nobody knows this rule.

25. Interrogative Pronouns and Adjectives

1. The interrogative pronoun *chi* refers to persons, and corresponds to *who* or *whom* or *which,* as illustrated by the three examples following:

Chi vi scrive?	Who writes to you?
Chi vediamo?	Whom do we see?
Chi di noi ha parlato?	Which of us has talked?

2. *Che* or *che cosa* translate *what:*

Che facciamo?	What are we doing?
Che cosa leggete?	What are you reading?

3. The two interrogative adjectives *quale* and *che* mean *which, what:*

Quale dei due giornali compra Lei?	Which of the two newspapers do you buy?
Che colore desiderate?	What color do you wish?

26. Relative Pronouns

chi	he who, him who
che	who, whom, that, which
cui	(used with prepositions)
di cui	of whom, of which
in cui	in which
Chi studia impara.	He who studies, learns.
l'uomo che ho visto	the man whom I saw
la donna di cui parlo	the woman of whom I speak

1. che: (undeclinable) For masculine, feminine, singular, plural; for persons, animals, things. Do not use this pronoun if there is a preposition.

2. il quale, la quale, i quali, le quali: For persons, animals, things, with the same English meanings as *che;* can be used with or without prepositions.

3. cui: (undeclinable) Masculine, feminine, singular, plural; for persons, animals, things; is always used with a preposition.

27. Personal Pronouns

Pronouns have different forms depending on whether they are:

1. the subject of a verb
2. the direct object of a verb
3. the indirect object of a verb
4. used after a preposition
5. used with reflexive verbs

1. The subject pronouns are:

SINGULAR

io	I
tu	you *(fam.)*
lui	he
lei	she
Lei	you *(pol.)*
esso	it (*masc.*)
essa	it (*fem.*)

PLURAL

noi	we
voi	you *(fam. plur.)*
loro	they (*masc.*)
loro	they (*fem.*)
Loro	you *(polite plur.)*

It is not necessary to use subject pronouns as the verb ending indicates who is speaking or being spoken about.

2. The direct object pronouns are:

mi	me
ti	you
lo	him, it
la	her, it, you
ci	us
vi	you

li	them, you
le	them, you

Ci vede.	He sees us.
Lo scrive.	He writes it.

3. The indirect object pronouns are:

mi	to me
ti	to you
gli	to him
le	to her, to you
ci	to us
vi	to you
loro	to them, to you

Lui mi scrive una lettera.	He is writing me a letter.
Io ti regalo una bambola.	I am giving you a doll.
Noi parliamo loro.	We speak to them.

4. The pronouns used after a preposition are:

me	me
te	you
lui	him
lei	her, you
noi	us
voi	you
loro	them, you

Io verrò con te.	I will come with you.
Lui parla sempre di lei.	He always speaks about her.

5. The reflexive pronouns are:

mi	myself
ti	yourself
si	himself, herself, itself, yourself
ci	ourselves

vi	yourselves
si	themselves, yourselves
Io mi lavo.	I wash myself.
Noi ci diamo la mano.	We shake hands.
Loro si alzano.	They get up.

28. Position of Pronouns

1. Pronouns are written as separate words, except with the imperative, infinitive, and gerund, where they follow the verbal form and are written as one word with it:

Ditelo.	Say it.
Fatemi un favore.	Do me a favor.
facendovi ...	doing it ...
chiamandolo	calling him
scriverle una lettera	to write her a letter
dopo avermi chiamato	after having called me

2. In the imperative, when the polite form is used, the pronouns are never attached to the verb:

Mi faccia un favore.	Do me a favor.

3. Some verbs of one syllable in the imperative double the initial consonant of the pronoun:

Dimmi una cosa.	Tell me one thing.
Facci una cortesia.	Do us a favor.

4. In the compound infinitive the pronoun is generally attached to the auxiliary:

Credo di averti dato tutto.	I think I gave you everything.

The simple infinitive drops the final *e* before the pronoun:

leggere un articolo	to read an article
leggerti un articolo	to read you an article

5. When two object pronouns are used with the same verb, the indirect precedes the direct:

Io te lo voglio dire.	I want to tell it to you.

Observe the following changes in the pronouns which occur in this case:

The *i* in *mi, ti, ci, vi, si* changes to *e* before *lo, la, le, li, ne,* while *gli* takes an additional *e* and is written as one word with the following pronoun. *Le* also becomes *glie* before *lo, la, li, le, ne:*

Ce lo dà.	He gives it to us.
Glielo mando a casa.	I send it home to him (to her, to you).
Glielo dicono.	They tell it to him (to her, to you).

29. Ne

1. Used as a pronoun meaning *of him, of her, of them, of it:*

Parla lei del mio amico?	Are you talking of my friend?
Sì,ne parlo.	Yes, I am talking of him.
Parliamo noi di questa cosa?	Are we talking of this thing?
Sì, ne parliamo.	Yes, we are talking of it.

2. Used as a partitive meaning “some” or “any”:

Mangi la signorina del pesce?	Does the young lady eat some fish?
Sì, ne mangia.	Yes, she does (eat some).

3. Used as an adverb of place, meaning *from* or *out of:*

Gli studenti escono dalla classe?	Are the students coming out from the class?
Sì, ne escono.	Yes, they are (coming out).

30. Si

1. Si can be used as a reflexive pronoun:

Lui si lava.	He washes himself.
Loro si lavano.	They wash themselves.

2. *Si* is used as an impersonal pronoun:

Non sempre si riflette su quel che si dice.	Not always does one ponder over what one says.
Qui si mangia bene.	Here one eats well.

3. *Si* is sometimes used to translate the English passive:

Come si manda questa lettera?	How is this letter sent?

31. Adverbs

1. Many adverbs end in *-mente:*

caramente	dearly
dolcemente	sweetly

These adverbs are easily formed; take the feminine singular form of the adjective and add *-mente.* For instance, "dear" = *caro, cara, cari, care*; the feminine singular is *cara,* and so the adverb will be *caramente.* "Sweet" is *dolce, dolci* (there is no difference between the masculine and feminine); the feminine singular is *dolce,* and so the adverb will be *dolcemente.*

2. Adjectives ending in *-le* or *-re,* if the *l* or *r* is preceded by a vowel, drop the final *e* before *-mente;* thus the adverb corresponding to *facile* is *facilmente* (easily);

celere (fast) becomes *celermente* (fast, *adv.*). The adverbs corresponding to *buono* (good) and *cattivo* (bad) are *bene* and *male.*

3. Adverbs may have a comparative and superlative form: *Caramente, più caramente, molto caramente,* or *carissimamente.*

Observe these irregular comparative and superlative forms of adverbs:

meglio	better
peggio	worse
maggiormente	more greatly
massimamente	very greatly
minimamente	in the least
ottimamente	very well
pessimamente	very bad

32. Prepositions

1. The most common prepositions in Italian are:

di	of
a	at to
da	from
in	in
con	with
su, sopra	above
per	through, by means of, on
tra, fra	between, among

2. When used in connection with the definite article, they are often contracted. Here are the most common of these combinations:

di + il = del	a + *il = al*
di + lo = dello	a + *lo = allo*

di + la = della	*a + la = alla*
di + l' = dell'	*a + l' = all'*
	a + i = ai
di + i = dei	*a + gli = agli*
di + gli = degli	*a + le = alle*
di + le = delle	
con + il = col	*sul + il = sul*
con + i = coi	*su + la = sulla*
	su + lo = sullo
	su + gli = sugli
	su + i = sui

Io ho del denaro.	I have some money.
il cavallo dello zio	the uncle's horse
Io regalo un dollaro al ragazzo.	I give a dollar to the boy.
Il professore risponde agli studenti.	The professor answers the students.

33. Negation

1. *Non* (not) comes before the verb:

Io non vedo.	I don't see.
Lui non parla.	He isn't speaking.

2. Nothing, never, no one:

Non vedo nulla.	I see nothing.
Non vado mai.	I never go.
Non viene nessuno.	No one comes.

If the negative pronoun begins the sentence, *non* is not used.

Nessuno viene.	No one comes.

34. Question Words

Che?	What?
Che cosa?	What?
Perchè?	Why?
Come?	How?
Quanto?	How much?
Quando?	When?
Dove?	Where?
Quale?	Which?

35. The Tenses of the Verb

A. Italian verbs are divided into three classes (conjugations) according to their infinitives:

Class I—*parlare, amare*
Class II—*scrivere, temere*
Class III—*partire, sentire*

1. The Present:

To form the present tense, take off the infinitive ending (*-are, -ere, -ire*) and add the following present tense endings:

First Conj. (I)	Second Conj. (II)	Third Conj. (III)
-o	*-o*	*-o*
-i	*-i*	*-i*
-a	*-e*	*-e*
-iamo	*-iamo*	*-iamo*
-ate	*-ete*	*-ite*
-ano	*-ono*	*-ono*

The present tense can be translated in several ways:

Io parlo italiano	I speak Italian. I am speaking Italian. I do speak Italian.

2. The Imperfect:

I.	II.	III.
-avo	*-evo*	*-ivo*
-avi	*-evi*	*-ivi*
-ava	*-eva*	*-iva*
-avamo	*-evamo*	*-ivamo*
-avate	*-evate*	*-ivate*
-avano	*-evano*	*-ivano*

The imperfect is used:

a. To indicate continued or customary action in the past:

Quando ero a Roma andavo sempre a visitare i musei.	When I was in Rome I was always visiting the museums.
Lo incontravo ogni giorno.	I used to meet him every day.

b. To indicate what was happening when something else happened:

Lui scriveva quando ella entrò.	He was writing when she entered.

3. The Future:

The future of regular verbs is formed by adding to the infinitive (after the final *e* is dropped) the endings *-ò; -ai; -à; -emo; -ete; -anno.* For the first conjugation, the *a* of the infinitive changes to *e.*

The future generally expresses actions which will take place in the future:

Lo comprerò.	I'll buy it.
Andrò domani.	I'll go tomorrow.

Sometimes it expresses probability or conjecture:

Che ora sarà?	What time can it be? What time do you think it must be?
Sarà l'una.	It must be almost one.
Starà mangiando ora.	He's probably eating now.

4. *Passato remoto* (preterit, past definite):
This tense indicates an action that happened in a period of time completely finished now:

Romolo fondò Roma.	Romulus founded Rome.
Dante nacque nel 1265.	Dante was born in 1265.
Garibaldi combattè per l'unità d'Italia.	Garibaldi fought for the unity of Italy.

5. *Passato prossimo* (compound past):
The *passato prossimo* is formed by adding the past participle to the present indicative of *avere* or *essere.* It is used to indicate a past action and corresponds to the English preterit or present perfect:

Io ho finito il mio avoro.	I finished my work. (I have finished my work.)
L'hai visto?	Have you seen him?
Sono arrivati.	They arrived.

6. The past perfect tense is formed by adding the past participle to the imperfect of *avere* or *essere.* It translates the English past perfect:

Lui l'aveva fatto.	He had done it.

7. The *trapassato remoto* (preterit perfect) is formed by adding the past participle to the past definite of *avere* or *essere.* It is used to indicate an event that had happened just before another event:

Quando usci ebbe finito.	When he went out, he had finished.

8. The future perfect tense is formed by adding the past participle to the future of *avere* or *essere.* It translates to the English future perfect:

Lui avrà finito presto.	He will soon have finished.

Sometimes it indicates probability:

Quando lui avrà finito, andra a casa.	When he has finished, he will go home.
Lui sara stato ammalato.	He probably was sick.

B. Complete conjugation of a sample verb from each class:

Amare (First Conjugation): to love, like

INDICATIVE

PRESENT	IMPERFECT
io amo	*io amavo*
tu ami	*tu amavi*
lui ama	*lui amava*
noi amiamo	*noi amavamo*
voi amate	*voi amavate*
loro amano	*loro amavano*

FUTURE	PRESENT PERFECT
io amerò	*io hoi amato*
tu amerai	*tu hai amato*
lui amerà	*lui ha amato*
noi ameremo	*noi abbiamo amato*
voi amerete	*voi avete amato*
loro ameranno	*loro hanno amato*

PRETERIT	PAST PERFECT
io amai	*io avevo amato*
tu amasti	*tu avevi amato*
lui amò	*lui aveva amato*
noi amammo	*noi avevamo amato*

voi amaste
loro amarono

voi avevate amato
loro avevano amato

PRETERIT PERFECT
io ebbi amato
tu avesti amato
lui ebbe amato
noi avemmo amato
voi aveste amato
loro ebbero amato

FUTURE PERFECT
io avrò amato
tu avrai amato
lui avrà amato
noi avremo amato
voi avrete amato
loro avranno amato

SUBJUNCTIVE

PRESENT
io ami
tu ami
lui ami
noi amiamo
voi amiate
loro amino

IMPERFECT
io amassi
tu amassi
lui amasse
noi amassimo
voi amaste
loro amassero

PERFECT
io abbia amato
tu abbia amato
lui abbia amato
noi abbiamo amato
voi abbiate amato
lui abbiano amato

PAST PERFECT
io avessi amato
tu avessi amato
lui avesse amato
noi avessimo amato
voi aveste amato
loro avessero amato

IMPERATIVE

PRESENT
ama (tu)
ami (lei)
amiamo (noi)
amate (voi)
amino (loro)

CONDITIONAL

PRESENT	PERFECT
io amerei	*io avrei amato*
tu ameresti	*tu avresti amato*
lui amerebbe	*lui avrebbe amato*
noi ameremmo	*noi avremmo amato*
voi amereste	*voi avreste amato*
loro amerebbero	*loro avrebbero amato*

INFINITIVES

PRESENT	PERFECT
amare	*avere amato*

PARTICIPLES

PRESENT	PERFECT
amante	*amato*

GERUNDS

PRESENT	PERFECT
amando	*avendo amato*

Temere (Second Conjugation): to fear

INDICATIVE

PRESENT	IMPERFECT
io temo	*io temevo*
tu temi	*tu temevi*
lui teme	*lui temeva*
noi temiamo	*noi temevamo*
voi temete	*voi temevate*
loro temono	*loro temevano*

FUTURE	PRESENT PERFECT
io temerò	*io ho temuto*
tu temerai	*tu hai temuto*
lui temerà	*lui ha temuto*

noi temeremo
voi temerete
loro temeranno

noi abbiamo temuto
voi avete temuto
loro hanno temuto

PRETERIT
io temei (or -etti)
tu temesti
lui temè (or -ette)
noi tememmo
voi temeste
loro temerono (or -ettero)

PAST PERFECT
io avevo temuto
tu avevi temuto
lui aveva temuto
noi avevamo temuto
voi avevate temuto
loro avevano temuto

PRETERIT PERFECT
io ebbi temuto
tu avesti temuto
lui ebbe temuto
noi avemmo temuto
voi aveste temuto
loro ebbero temuto

FUTURE PERFECT
io avrò temuto
tu avrai temuto
lui avrà temuto
noi avremo temuto
voi avrete temuto
loro avranno temuto

SUBJUNCTIVE

PRESENT
io tema
tu tema
lui tema
noi temiamo
voi temiate
loro temano

IMPERFECT
io temessi
tu temessi
lui temesse
noi temessimo
voi temeste
loro temessero

PERFECT
io abbia temuto
tu abbia temuto
lui abbia temuto
noi abbiamo temuto
voi abbiate temuto
loro abbiano temuto

PAST PERFECT
io avessi temuto
tu avessi temuto
lui avesse temuto
noi avessimo temuto
voi aveste temuto
loro avessero temuto

IMPERATIVE

PRESENT
temi (tu)
tema (lei)
temiamo (noi)
temete (voi)
temano (loro)

CONDITIONAL

PRESENT	PERFECT
io temerei	*io avrei temuto*
tu temeresti	*tu avresti temuto*
lui temerebbe	*lui avrebbe temuto*
noi temeremmo	*noi avremmo temuto*
voi temereste	*voi avreste temuto*
loro temerebbero	*loro avrebbero temuto*

INFINITIVES

PRESENT	PERFECT
temere	*aver temuto*

PARTICIPLES

PRESENT	PERFECT
temente	*temuto*

GERUNDS

PRESENT	PERFECT
temendo	*avendo temuto*

Sentire (Third Conjugation):

INDICATIVE

PRESENT	IMPERFECT
io sento	*io sentivo*
tu senti	*tu sentivi*
lui sente	*lui sentiva*

noi sentiamo
voi sentite
loro sentono

noi sentivamo
voi sentivate
loro sentivano

FUTURE
io sentirò
tu sentirai
lui sentirà
noi sentiremo
voi sentirete
loro sentiranno

PRESENT PERFECT
io ho sentito
tu hai sentito
lui ha sentito
noi avevamo sentito
voi avete sentito
loro hanno sentito

PRETERIT
io sentii
tu sentisti
lui senti
noi sentimmo
voi sentiste
loro sentirono

PAST PERFECT
io avevo sentito
tu avevi sentito
lui aveva sentito
noi avevamo sentito
voi avevate sentito
loro avevano sentito

PRETERIT PERFECT
io ebbi sentito
tu avesti sentito
lui ebbe sentito
noi avemmo sentito
voi aveste sentito
loro ebbero sentito

FUTURE PERFECT
io avrò sentito
tu avrai sentito
lui avrà sentito
noi avremo sentito
voi avrete sentito
loro avranno sentito

SUBJUNCTIVE

PRESENT
io senta
tu senta
lui senta
noi sentiamo
voi sentiate
loro sentano

IMPERFECT
io sentissi
tu sentissi
lui sentisse
noi sentissimo
voi sentiste
loro sentissero

PERFECT	PAST PERFECT
io abbia sentito	*io avessi sentito*
tu abbia sentito	*tu avessi sentito*
lui abbia sentito	*lui avesse sentito*
noi abbiamo sentito	*noi avessimo sentito*
voi abbiate sentito	*voi aveste sentito*
loro abbiano sentito	*loro avessero sentito*

IMPERATIVE

PRESENT
senti (tu)
senta (lei)
sentiamo (noi)
sentite (voi)
sentano (loro)

CONDITIONAL

PRESENT	PERFECT
io sentirei	*io avrei sentito*
tu sentiresti	*tu avresti sentito*
lui sentirebbe	*lui avrebbe sentito*
noi sentiremmo	*noi avremmo sentito*
voi sentireste	*voi avreste sentito*
loro sentirebbero	*loro avrebbero sentito*

INFINITIVES

PRESENT	PERFECT
sentire	*aver sentito*

PARTICIPLES

PRESENT	PERFECT
sentente	*sentito*

GERUNDS

PRESENT	PERFECT
sentendo	*avendo sentito*

36. The Past Participle

1. The past participle ends in:

-ato, (-ata, -ati, -ate) (for the First Conjugation)	*parl -ato*
-uto (for the Second Conjugation)	*bev -uto*
-ito (for the Third Conjugation)	*part -ito*

2. The past participle used with *essere* agrees with the subject of the verb:

è andato	he left
sono andate	they (*fem.*) left

3. The past participle used with *avere* generally agrees with the preceding direct object:

i libri che lei ha comprati	the books that she bought
i libri che lui ha comprati	the books that he bought

37. Use of the Auxiliaries

The most common intransitive verbs that are conjugated with the verb *essere* in the compound tenses are the following:

andare, arrivare, scendere, entrare, salire, morire, nascere, partire, restare, ritornare, uscire, cadere, venire, rivenire.

Io sono venuto.	I have come.
Egli è arrivato.	He has arrived.
Noi siamo partiti.	We have left.

Reflexive verbs form their past tenses with *essere.* If there is a direct object, generally the past participle agrees with it, and not with the subject:

La signorina si è rotto il braccio.	The young lady broke her arm.

The past tenses of passive constructions are formed with *essere:*

Il ragazzo è amato.	The boy is loved.
La ragazza è stata amata.	The girl has been loved.
I ragazzi furono amati.	The boys were loved.
Le ragazze saranno amate.	The girls will be loved.

Sometimes the verb *venire* is used instead of *essere* in a passive construction:

La poesia è letta dal maestro.	The poem is read by the teacher.
La poesia viene letta dal maestro.	The poem is read by the teacher.

38. The Progressive Present

Io fumo means "I smoke" or "I am smoking," but there is also a special way of translating "I am smoking": *Io sto fumando.* In other words, Italian uses the verb *stare* with the present gerund of the main verb:

Noi stiamo leggendo.	We are reading.
Lui stava scrivendo.	He was writing.

This form is generally used only in the simple tenses.

39. SUBJUNCTIVE

A. Formation

1. The Present Tense

a. First Conjugation: By dropping the *-are* from the infinitive, and adding *-i, -i, -i, -iamo, -iate, -ino.*

Penso che lui parli troppo.	I think (that) he speaks too much.

b. Second and Third Conjugation: By dropping the -*ere* and *-ire,* and adding *-a, -a, -a, -iamo, -iate, -iano.*

Sebbene Lei scriva in fretta non fa errori.	Although you write fast, you make no mistakes.

2. The Imperfect Tense

a. First Conjugation: By dropping the *-are,* and adding *-assi, -assi, -asse, -assimo, -aste, -assero.*

Credevo che il ragazzo lavorasse molto.	I thought (that) the boy was working hard.

b. Second Conjugation: By dropping the *-ere,* and adding *-essi,-essi, -esse, -essimo, -este, -essero.*

Prima che le signorina scrivesse la lettera il padre la chiamo.	Before the girl could write the letter her father called her.

c. Third Conjugation: By dropping the *-ire,* and adding *-issi, -issi, -isse, -issimo, -iste, -issero.*

Ero del parere che il mio amico si sentisse male.	I was under the impression that my friend did not feel well.

3. The Compound Tenses (Perfect and Past Perfect)

They are formed with the present and imperfect of the subjunctive of "to have" and "to be," and the past participle.

Credo che gli studenti abbiano finito la lezione.	I think (that) the students have finished the lesson.
Era possibile che i mei amici fossero già arrivati in città.	It was possible that my friends had already arrived in town.

B. Uses of the Subjunctive

The subjunctive mood expresses doubt, uncertainity, hope, fear, desire, supposition, possibility, probability, granting, etc. For this reason, it is mostly found in clauses dependent upon another verb.

1. In a few cases the subjunctive is used alone. The most common ones are:

a. In exhortations:

Facciamo cosi.	Let us do so.
Pensiamo come fare queste cose.	Let us think how to do these things.

b. To express a wish or desire:

Siate felici!	May you be happy!

2. The subjunctive is used in dependent clauses in the following ways:

a. After verbs expressing hope, wish, desire, command, doubt:

Voglio che tu ci vada.	I want you to go there.

b. After verbs expressing an opinion (*penso, credo*):

Penso che sia vero.	I think it is true.

c. After expressions made with a form of *essere* and an adjective or an adverb (*è necessario, è facile, è possibile*), or some impersonal expressions like *bisogna, importa, etc.*:

È necessario che io parta subito.	It is necessary that I leave immediately.
È impossibile che noi veniamo questa sera.	It is impossible for us to come this evening.

d. After some conjunctions--*sebbene, quantunque, per quanto, benchè, affinchè, prima che* (subjunctive to express a possibility; indicative to express a fact):

Sebbene non sia guarito, devo uscire.	Although I am not well yet, I must go out.
Benche te l'abbia già detto, ricordati di andare alla Posta.	Although I told you already, remember to go to the Post Office.

40. CONDITIONAL

The conditional is formed:

1. In the present tense:

a. First and Second Conjugations: By dropping the *-are,* or *-ere,* and adding *-erei, -ereste, -erebbe, -eremmo, -ereste, -erebbero.*

La signora parlerebbe molto, se potesse.	The lady would speak a lot if she could.

b. Third Conjugation: By dropping the *-ire,* and adding *-irei, -iresti, -irebbe, -iremmo, -ireste, -irebbero.*

Il signore si sentirebbe bene, se prendesse le pillole.	The gentleman would feel well if he took the pills.

2. In the past tense:

By using the present conditional of "to have" or "to be" and the past participle.

Mio cugino non avrebbe investito il suo denaro in questo, se l'avesse saputo primo.	My cousin would not have invested his money in this, if he had known it before.

41. "If" Clauses

An "if" clause can express:

1. *Reality.* In this case the indicative is used:

Se oggi piove, non uscirò.	If it rains today, I won't go out.

2. *Possibility.* The imperfect subjunctive and the conditional present are used to express possibility in the present:

Se tu leggessi impareresti.	If you read, you would learn. (The idea is that it is possible that you may read and so you may learn.)

The past perfect subjunctive and the past conditional are used to express a possibility in the past:

Se tu avessi letto avresti imparato.	If you had read, you would have learned. (The idea is that you might have read and so might have learned.)

3. *Impossibility* or *unreality.* Use the same construction as in number 2; the only difference is that we know that the condition cannot be fulfilled.

Se l'uomo vivesse mille anni, imparerebbe molte cose.	If a man lived 1,000 years, he would learn many things. (But it's a fact that people don't live 1,000 years, and so don't learn many things.)
Se io avessi studiato quando ero giovane, avrei fatto un gran piacere ai miei genitori.	If I had studied when I was young, I would have given great pleasure to my parents. (But it's a fact that I did not study, and so I did not bring great pleasure to my parents.)

42. Imperative

The forms of the imperative are normally taken from the present indicative:

leggi	read
leggiamo	let us read
leggete	read

For the First Conjugation, however, note:

canta	sing

The polite forms of the imperative are taken from the present subjunctive:

canti	sing
cantino	sing
legga	read
leggano	read

43. "To Be" and "To Have"

Essere and *avere*, "to be" and "to have," are very irregular. For your convenience here are their conjugations.

ESSERE:

INDICATIVE

PRESENT	PRETERIT
io sono	*io fui*
tu sei	*tu fosti*
lui è	*lui fu*
noi siamo	*noi fummo*
voi siete	*voi foste*
loro sono	*loro furono*

IMPERFECT	PAST PERFECT
io ero	*io ero stato/a*
tu eri	*tu eri stato/a*
lui era	*lui era stato*
noi eravamo	*noi eravamo stati/e*
voi eravate	*voi eravate stati/e*
loro erano	*erano stati/e*

FUTURE	PRETERIT PERFECT
io sarò	*io fui stato/a*
tu sarai	*tu fosti stato/a*

lui sarà
noi saremo
voi sarete
loro saranno

lui fu stato
noi fummo stati/e
voi foste stati/e
loro furono stati/e

PRESENT PERFECT
io sono stato/a
tu sei stato/a
lui è stato
noi siamo stati/e
voi siete stati/e
loro sono stati/e

FUTURE PERFECT
io sarò stato/a
tu sarai stato/a
lui sarà stato
noi saremo stati/e
voi sarete stati/e
loro saranno stati/e

SUBJUNCTIVE

PRESENT
io sia
tu sia
lui sia
noi siamo
voi siate
loro siano

IMPERFECT
io fossi
tu fossi
lui fosse
noi fossimo
voi foste
loro fossero

PERFECT
io sia stato/a
tu sia stato/a
lui sia stato
noi siamo stati/e
voi siate stati/e
loro siano stati/e

PAST PERFECT
io fossi stato/a
tu fossi stato/a
lui fosse stato
noi fossimo stati/e
voi foste stati/e
loro fossero stati/e

IMPERATIVE

PRESENT
sii (tu)
sia (lei)
siamo (noi)
siate (voi)
siano (loro)

CONDITIONAL

PRESENT
io sarei

PERFECT
io sarei stato/a

tu saresti	*tu saresti stato/a*
lui sarebbe	*lui sarebbe stato*
noi saremmo	*noi saremmo stati/e*
voi sareste	*voi sareste stati/e*
loro sarebbero	*loro sarebbero stati/e*

INFINITIVE

PRESENT	PERFECT
essere	*essere stato/a/i/e*

PARTICIPLE

	PERFECT
	stato/a/i/e

GERUND

PRESENT	PERFECT
essendo	*essendo stato/a/i/e*

AVERE:

INDICATIVE

PRESENT	PRETERIT
io ho	*io ebbi*
tu hai	*tu avesti*
lui ha	*lui ebbe*
noi abbiamo	*noi avemmo*
voi avete	*voi aveste*
loro hanno	*loro ebbero*

IMPERFECT	PAST PERFECT
io avevo	*io avevo avuto*
tu avevi	*tu avevi avuto*
lui aveva	*lui aveva avuto*
noi avevamo	*noi avevamo avuto*
voi avevate	*voi avevate avuto*
loro avevano	*loro avevano avuto*

FUTURE	PRETERIT PERFECT
io avrò	*io ebbi avuto*
tu avrai	*tu avesti avuto*
lui avrà	*lui ebbi avuto*
noi avremo	*noi avemmo avuto*

voi avrete
loro avranno

voi aveste avuto
loro ebbero avuto

PRESENT PERFECT
io ho avuto
tu hai avuto
lui ha avuto
noi abbiamo avuto
voi avete avuto
loro hanno avuto

FUTURE PERFECT
io avrò avuto
tu avrai avuto
lui avrà avuto
noi avremo avuto
voi avrete avuto
loro avranno avuto

SUBJUNCTIVE

PRESENT
io abbia
tu abbia
lui abbia
noi abbiamo
vi abbiate
loro abbiano

IMPERFECT
io avessi
tu avessi
noi avessimo
voi aveste
lui avesse
loro avessero

PERFECT
io abbia avuto
tu abbia avuto
lui abbia avuto
noi abbiamo avuto
voi abbiate avuto
loro abbiano avuto

PAST PERFECT
io avessi avuto
tu avessi avuto
lui avesse avuto
noi avessimo avuto
voi aveste avuto
loro avessero avuto

IMPERATIVE

PRESENT
abbi (tu)
abbia (Lei)
abbiamo (noi)
abbiate (voi)
abbiaus (loro)

CONDITIONAL

PRESENT
io avrei
tu avresti

PERFECT
io avrei avuto
nci avremmo avuto

lui avrebbe	*tu avresti avuto*
noi avremmo	*lui avrebbe avuto*
voi avreste	*voi avreste avuto*
loro avrebbero	*loro avrebbero avuto*

INFINITIVE

PRESENT	PERFECT
avere	*avere avuto*

PARTICIPLES

PRESENT	PERFECT
avente	*avuto*

GERUND

PRESENT	PERFECT
avendo	*avendo avuto*

44. Some Irregular Verbs

(Only irregular tenses are indicated. Other tenses follow the regular pattern of the conjugation as shown in the tenses of the verb.)

Andare = to go
Ind. pres.: *vado, vai, va, andiamo, andate, vanno.*
Future: *andrò, andrai, andrà, andremo, andrete, andranno.*
Subj. pres.: *vada, vada, vada, andiamo, andiate, vadano.*
Imperative: *va', vada, andiamo, andate, vadano.*
Cond. pres.: *andrei, andresti, andrebbe, andremmo,* etc.

Bere = to drink
Ind. pres.: *bevo, bevi, beve, beviamo, bevete, bevono.*
Imperfect: *bevevo, bevevi,* etc.
Preterit: *bevvi, bevesti, beve, bevemmo, beveste, bevvero.*
Future: *berrò, berrai, berrà, berremo, berrete, berrano.*
Subj. imp.: *bevessi,* etc.

Cond. pres.: *berrei, berresti, berrebbe,* etc.
Past part.: *bevuto.*

Cadere = to fall
Future: *cadrò, cadrai, cadrà, cadremo, cadrete, cadranno.*
Preterit: *caddi, cadesti, cadde, cademmo, cadeste, caddero.*
Cond. pres.: *cadrei, cadresti, cadrebbe,* etc.

Chiedere = to ask
Preterit: *chiesi, chiedesti, chiese, chiedemmo, chiedeste, chiesero.*
Past part.: *chiesto*

Chiudere = to shut
Preterit: *chiusi, chiudesti, chiuse, chiudemmo, chiudeste, chiusero.*
Past part.: *chiuso.*

Conoscere = to know
Preterit: *conobbi, conoscesti, conobbe, conoscemmo, conosceste, conobbero.*
Past part.: *conosciuto.*

Cuocere = to cook
Ind. pres.: *cuocio, cuoci, cuoce, cociamo, cocete, cuociono.*
Preterit: *cossi, cocesti, cosse, cocemmo, coceste, cossero.*
Subj. pres.: *cuocia or cocia,* etc.
Imperative: *cuoci, cuocia,* etc.
Past part.: *cotto.*

Dare = to give
Ind. pres.: *do, dai, dà, diamo, date, danno.*
Preterit: *diedi* or *detti, desti, diede* or *dette, demmo, deste, dettero* or *diedero.*
Subj. pres.: *dia, dia, dia, diamo, diate, diano.*
Subj. imper.: *dessi, dessi, desse, dessimo, deste, dessero.*
Imperative: *da', dia, diamo, date, diano.*
Past part.: *dato.*

Dire = to say
Ind. pres.: *dico, dici, dice, diciamo, dite, dicono.*
Imperfect: *dicevo, dicevi,* etc.
Preterit: *dissi, dicesti, disse, dicemmo, diceste, dissero.*
Subj. pres.: *dica, dica, dica, diciamo, diciate, dicano.*
Subj. imper.: *dicessi, dicessi, dicesse, dicessimo, diceste, dicerssero.*
Imperative: *di, dica, diciamo, dite, dicano.*
Past part.: *detto.*

Dolere = to suffer, to ache
Ind. pres.: *dolgo, duoli, duole, doliamo, dolete, dolgono.*
Preterit: *dolsi, dolesti, dolse, dolemmo, doleste, dolsero.*
Future: *dorrò, dorrai, dorrà, dorremo, dorrete, dorranno.*
Subj. pres.: *dolga,* etc., *doliamo, doliate, dolgano.*
Cond. pres.: *dorrei, dorresti, dorrebbe,* etc.

Dovere = to owe, to be obliged
Ind. pres.: *devo* or *debbo, devi, deve, dobbiamo,* or *dovete, devono,* or *debbono.*
Future: *dovrò, dovrai, dovrà,* etc.
Subj. pres.: *deva* or *debba, deva* or *debba, deva* or *debba, dobbiamo, dobbiate, devano* or *debbano.*
Cond. pres.: *dovrei, dovresti, dovrebbe, dovremmo, dovreste, dovrebbero.*

Fare = to do
Ind. pres.: *faccio, fai, fa, facciamo, fate, fanno.*
Imperfect: *facevo, facevi,* etc.
Preterit: *feci, facesti, fece, facemmo, faceste, fecero.*
Subj. pres.: *faccia,* etc.
Subj. imp.: *facessi,* etc.
Imper. pres.: *fa', faccia,* etc.
Past part.: *fatto.*

Godere = to enjoy
Future: *goderò* or *godrò, godrai, godrà,* etc.
Cond. pres.: *godrei, godresti, godrebbe,* etc.

Leggere = to read
Preterit: *lessi, leggesti, lesse, leggemo, leggeste, lessero.*
Past part.: *letto.*

Mettere = to put
Preterit: *misi, mettesti, mise, mettemmo, metteste, misero.*
Past part.: *messo.*

Morire = to die
Ind. pres.: *muoio, muori, muore, moriamo, morite, muoiono.*
Future: *morirò* or *morrò,* etc.
Subj. pres.: *muoia,* etc.
Cond. pres.: *morirei or morrei,* etc.
Pres. part.: *morente.*
Past part.: *morto.*

Nascere = to be born
Preterit: *nacqui, nascesti, nacque, nascemmo, nasceste, nacquero.*
Past part.: *nato.*

Nuocere = to hurt, to harm
Ind. pres.: *nuoco, nuoci, nuoce, nociamo, nocete, nuocono.*
Preterit: *nocqui, nocesti, nocque, nocemmo, noceste, nocquero.*
Subj. pres.: *noccia, noccia, noccia, nocciamo, nocciate, nocciano.*
Past part.: *nociuto.*

Piacere = to please, to like
Ind. pres.: *piaccio, piaci, piace, piacciamo, piacete, piacciono.*
Preterit: *piacqui, piacesti, piacque, piacemmo, piaceste,* etc.
Subj. pres.: *piaccia,* etc.
Past part.: *piaciuto.*

Piovere = to rain
Preterit: *piovve,* etc.
Past part.: *piovuto.*

Potere = to be able
Ind. pres.: *posso, puoi, può, possiamo, potete, possono.*
Future: *potrò, potrai, potrà,* etc.
Subj. pres.: *possa, possa, possa, possiamo, possiate, possano.*
Cond. pres.: *potrei, portresti, potrebbe,* etc.

Ridere = to laugh
Preterit: *risi, ridesti, rise, ridemmo, rideste, risero.*
Past part.: *riso.*

Rimanere = to stay
Ind. pres.: *rimango, rimani, rimane, rimaniamo, rimanete, rimangono.*
Preterit: *rimasi, rimanesti, rimase, rimanemmo, rimaneste, rimasero.*
Future: *rimarrò, rimarrai, rimarrà, rimarremo,* etc.
Subj. pres.: *rimanga,* etc.
Cond. pres.: *rimarrei, rimarresti, rimarrebbe,* etc.
Past part.: *rimasto.*

Rispondere = to answer
Preterit: *risposi, rispondesti, rispose, rispondemmo, rispondeste, risposero.*
Past part.: *risposto.*

Salire = to go up, to climb
Ind. pres.: *salgo, sali, sale, saliamo, salite, salgono.*
Subj. pres.: *salga,* etc.
Imperative: *sali, salga, saliamo, salite, salgano.*
Past part.: *salito.*

Sapere = to know
Ind. pres.: *so, sai, sa, sappiamo, sapete, sanno.*
Future: *saprò, saprai, saprà,* etc.
Preterit: *seppi, sapesti, seppe, sapemmo, sapeste, seppero.*
Subj. pres.: *sappia,* etc.
Imperative: *sappi, sappia,* etc.
Cond. pres.: *saprei, sapresti, saprebbe,* etc.
Past part.: *saputo.*

Scegliere = to choose, select
Ind. pres.: *scelgo, scegli, sceglie, scegliamo, scegliete, scelgono.*
Preterit: *scelsi,* etc.
Subj. pres.: *scelga,* etc.
Imperative: *scegli, scelga, scegliamo, scegliete, scelgano.*
Past part.: *scelto*

Scendere = to go down, descend
Preterit: *scesi, scendeste, scese, scendemmo, scendeste, scesero.*
Past part.: *sceso.*

Scrivere = to write
Preterit: *scrissi, scrivesti, scrisse, scrivemmo, scriveste, scrissero.*
Past part.: *scritto.*

Sedere = to sit
Ind. pres.: *siedo* or *seggo, siedi, siede, sediamo, sedete, siedono* or *seggono.*
Subj. pres.: *sieda* or *segga,* etc.
Imperative: *siedi, sieda* or *segga,* etc.

Stare = to stay; to remain (to be)
Ind. pres.: *sto, stai, sta, stiamo, state, stanno.*
Preterit: *stetti, stesti, stette, stemmo, steste, stettero.*
Future: *starò, starai, starà,* etc.
Subj. pres.: *stia, stia, stia, stiamo, stiate, stiano.*
Subj. imper.: *stessi, stessi, stesse, stessimo, steste, stessero.*
Imperative: *sta', stia,* etc.
Cond. pres.: *starei, staresti, starebbe,* etc.
Past part.: *stato.*

Tacere = to be silent
Ind. pres.: *taccio, taci, tace, taciamo, tacete, tacciono.*
Preterit: *tacqui, tacesti, tacque,* etc.
Subj. pres.: *taccia, taccia, taccia, taciamo, taciate, tacciano.*
Imperative: *taci, taccia,* etc.
Past part.: *taciuto.*

Udire = to hear, listen
Ind. pres.: *odo, odi, ode, udiamo, udite, odono.*
Future: *udro, udrai, udra,* etc.
Subj. pres.: *oda,* etc.
Condit.: *udirei (udrei).*
Imperative: *odi, oda, udiamo, udite, odano.*

Uscire = to go out
Ind. pres.: *esco, esci, esce, usciamo, uscite, escono.*
Subj. pres.: *esca,* etc.
Imperative: *esci, esca, usciamo, uscite, escano.*

Vedere = to see
Ind. pres.: *vedo* or *veggo, vedi, vede, vediamo, vedete, vedono* or *veggono.*
Preterit: *vidi, vidésti, vide, videmmo, videste, videro.*
Future: *vedro,* etc.
Past part.: *veduto* or *visto.*

Venire = to come
Ind. pres.: *vengo, vieni, viene, veniamo, venite, vengono.*
Preterit: *venni, venisti, venne,* etc.
Future: *verrò, verrai, verrà, verremo,* etc.
Subj. pres.: *venga,* etc.
Imperative: *vieni, venga,* etc.
Cond. pres.: *verrei, verresti, verrebbe,* etc.
Pres. part.: *veniente.*
Past part.: *venuto.*

Vivere = to live
Preterit: *vissi, vivesti, visse, vivemmo, viveste, vissero.*
Future: *vivrò, vivrai, vivrà,* etc.
Cond. pres.: *vivrei, vivresti, vivrebbe,* etc.
Past part.: *vissuto.*

Volere = to want
Ind. pres.: *voglio, vuoi, vuole, vogliamo, volete, vogliono.*
Preterit: *volli, volesti, volle, volemmo, voleste, vollero.*

Future: *vorrò, vorrai, vorrà,* etc.
Subj. pres.: *voglia,* etc.
Cond. pres.: *vorrei, vorresti, vorrebbe,* etc.
Past part.: *voluto.*

LETTER WRITING

A. Formal Invitations and Acceptances
Inviti Formali

marzo 1993

Il signore e la signora Peretti hanno il piacere di annunciare il matrimonio della loro figlia Maria con il signor Giovanni Rossi, ed hanno l'onore di invitare la Signoria Vostra alla cerimonia che avrà luogo nella Chiesa di San Guiseppe, il sei di questo mese, alle ore dodici. Dopo la cerimonia un ricevimento sarà dato in onore degli sposi nella casa dei genitori della sposa.

March 1993

Mr. and Mrs. Peretti take pleasure in announcing the wedding of their daughter Maria to Mr. John Rossi, and have the honor of inviting you to the ceremony that will take place at the Church of St. Joseph, on the 6th of this month at 12 noon. There will be a reception for the newlyweds afterwards at the residence of the bride's parents.

marzo 1993

Il signore e la signora De Marchi hanno il piacere di invitare il signor Rossi e la sua gentile signora a cena lunedì prossimo, alle otto.

March 1993

Mr. and Mrs. De Marchi take pleasure in inviting Mr. and Mrs. Rossi to dinner next Monday at 8 o'clock.

marzo 1993

Il signore e la signora Martini hanno il piacere di invitare il signore e la signora Parisi al ricevimento in onore della loro figlia Anna, domenica sera, 19 marzo, alle ore nove.

March 1993
Mr. and Mrs. Martini take pleasure in inviting Mr. and Mrs. Parisi to a party given in honor of their daughter Anna, on Sunday evening, March 19, at nine o'clock.

RESPONSES *RISPOSTE*

Il signor Parisi e signora ringraziano per il cortese invito, felici di prendere parte al ricevimento del 19 marzo p.v.

Thank you for your kind invitation. We shall be honored to attend the reception on March 19th.

[Note: *p.v.* = *prossimo venturo,* which means "the next coming" (month). *c.m.* = *corrente mese,* which means "of this month" (the running month.)]

I coniugi Rossi accettano il gentile invito per lunedì prossimo e ringraziano sentitamente.

Mr. and Mrs. Rossi will be honored to have dinner with Mr. and Mrs. De Marchi next Monday. With kindest regards.

I coniugi Rossi ringraziano sentitamente il signore e la signora Peretti per il cortese invito, spiacenti che impegni precedenti non permettano loro di poter accettare.

Mr. and Mrs. Rossi thank Mr. and Mrs. Peretti for their kind invitation and regret that they are unable to come owing to a previous engagement.

B. Thank-You Notes
Biglietti Di Ringraziare

Roma, 5 marzo 1993

Cara Anna,

Poche righe soltanto per sapere come stai e per ringraziarti del bellissimo vaso che mi hai regalato. L'ho messo sul pianoforte, e ti assicuro che è bellissimo.

Spero di vederti domani al ricevimento di Angela. Sono sicura che la festa sarà molto divertente.

Mi auguro che la tua famiglia stia bene, come posso assicurarti della mia. Ti saluto affettuosamente.

Maria

March 5, 1993

Dear Anna,

This is just to say hello and also to let you know that I received the beautiful vase you sent me as a gift. I've put it on the piano and you can't imagine how nice it looks.

I hope to see you at Angela's party tomorrow. I think it's going to be a lot of fun.

I hope your family is all well. Everyone here is fine.

Affectionately,

Maria

C. Business Letters
Lettere commerciali

Cavatorta & Co.,
Via Veneto 125,
Roma—Italia

Ditta Marini e Figli
Via Nomentana 11,
Roma.

Roma, 2 aprile, 1993

Gentili Signori:

Abbiamo il piacere di presentarvi il portatore di questa lettera, signor Carlo Fontanesi, che è uno dei nostri agenti attualmente in vista alle principali città del vostro Paese. Inutile aggiungere che qualsiasi gentilezza sarà usata al signor Fontanesi sarà da noi gradita come un personale favore.

Ringraziandovi in anticipo, vi inviamo i nostri distinti saluti.

Cavatorta & Co.
il Presidente

Cavatorta & Co.
125 Veneto Street
Rome—Italy

(Firm) Marini & Sons
11 Nomentana Street
Rome.

April 2, 1993

Gentlemen:

We have the pleasure of introducing to you the bearer of this letter, Mr. Charles Fontanesi, one of our salesmen, who is visiting the principal cities of your country. Needless to add, we shall greatly appreciate any courtesy you extend to him. (It is needless to say to you that we shall consider any courtesy you extend to him as a personal favor.)

Thanking you in advance, we send our best regards.

Cavatorta & Co.

President

Milano, 3 marzo 1993
Signor Giulio Perri
direttore de "Il Mondo"
Via Montenapoleone 3,
Milano.

Gentile Signore:

Includo un assegno di L. 30.000 (trentamila) per un anno di abbonamento alla sua rivista.

Distintamente

Lucia Landi

Lucia Landi
Corso Vittorio Emanuele, 8
Roma.

March 3, 1993

Mr. Giulio Perri
Editor of *The World*
3 Montenapoleone Street
Milan.

Dear Sir:
Enclosed please find a check for $25.00 for a year's subscription to your magazine.

Very truly yours,
Lucia Landi

Lucia Landi
8 Corso Vittorio Emanuele
Rome.

D. Informal Letters
Lettere Informale

Caro Giuseppe,

Sono stato molto lieto di ricevere la tua ultima lettera. Prima di tutto desidero darti la grande notizia. Ho finalmente deciso di fare un viaggio fino a Roma, dove intendo rimanere tutto il mese di maggio. Anna verrà con me. Lei è molto felice che avrà cosi l'occasione di conoscere voi due. Cerca, perciò, di essere possibilmente libero, per allora.

Gli affari vanno bene, e spero che il buon vento continui. L'altro giorno ho visto Antonio, ed lui mi ha chiesto tue notizie.

Ti sarei grato se vorrai riservarci una camera all'albergo Nazionale. Scrivi presto. Saluti ad Elena.

tuo
Giovanni

Dear Joseph,

I was very happy to get your last letter. First of all, let me give you the big news. I have finally decided to make a trip to Rome, where I expect to spend all of May. Anna will come with me. She is extremely happy to be able to meet the two of you at last. Try therefore to be as free as you can then.

Business is good now, and I hope will keep that way (that the good wind will continue). I saw Anthony the other day and he asked me about you.

I'd be grateful to you if you would try to reserve a room for us at the National Hotel. Write soon. Give my regards to Helen.

Yours,
John

E. Forms of Salutations

Formal

Signore	Sir
Signora	Madam (Mrs.)
Signorina	Miss
Signor Professore	My dear Professor
Eccellentissimo	Your Excellency
Gentile Signor Rossi	My dear Mr. Rossi
Gentile Signora Rossi	My dear Mrs. Rossi
Gentile Signorina Rossi	My dear Miss Rossi

Informal

Caro Antonio	My dear Anthony
Cara Anna	My dear Anna
Mia amata	My beloved
Mio amato	My beloved, My dear
Carissimo Paolo	My very dear Paul
Carissima Giovanna	My very dear Jane

F. Forms of Complimentary Closings

Formal

1. *Gradisca i miei piu distinti saluti* (The *lei* form is used.)	Very truly yours. (Accept my most distinguished greetings.)
2. *Gradite i miei distinti saluti.* (The *voi* form is used.)	Very truly yours. (Accept my distinguished greetings.)
3. *Voglia gradire i miei sinceri saluti.* (The *lei* form is used.)	Yours truly. (Accept my sincere greetings.)

4. *Vogliate gradire miei cordiali saluti* (The *voi* form is used.)	Yours truly. (Accept my heartfelt greetings.)
5. *Devotissimi.* (Can be shortened to *Dev. mo.*) (The plural form is used.)	Yours truly. (Your very devoted.)
6. *Devotissimo* (Shortened to *Dev.mo.*) (The singular form is used.)	Yours truly. (Your very devoted.)

Informal

1. *Ricevete i nostri saluti.*	Very sincerely. (Receive our heartfelt greetings.)
2. *In attesa di vostre notizie vi invio i miei sinceri e cordiali saluti.*	Sincerely yours (Waiting for your news I send you my sincere and heartfelt greetings.)
3. *Sperando di ricevere presto tue notizie t'invio cordialissimi saluti.*	Sincerely yours. (Waiting to hear from you soon I send you my most heartfelt greetings.)
4. *Tuo amico.*	Sincerely. (Your friend.)
5. *Tua amica.*	Sincerely. (Your friend.)
6. *Affettuosissimo.* (Shortened to *Aff. mo*)	Affectionately yours. (Very affectionate.)
7. *Affettuosissima.* (Shortened to *Aff. ma*)	Affectionately yours (Very affectionate.)

8. *Affezionatissimo (Aff. mo)*	Affectionately yours. (Very affectionate.)
9. *Non altro vi invio cordiali saluti.*	Sincerely. (No more I send you heartfelt greetings.)
10. *Non altro t'invio cordiali saluti e abbracci.*	Sincerely. (No more I send you heartfelt greetings and embraces.)
11. *Con mille abbracci e baci.*	Love. (With a thousand embraces and kisses.)
12. *Abbracciandoti e baciandoti caramente.*	Love. (Embracing and kissing you dearly.)

G. Form of the Envelope

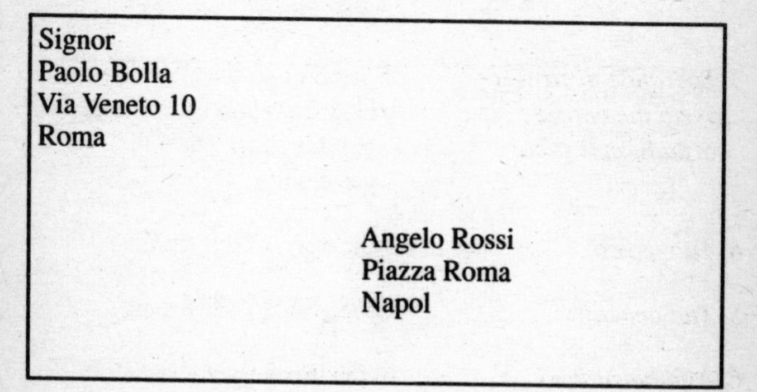
Signor
Paolo Bolla
Via Veneto 10
Roma

Angelo Rossi
Piazza Roma
Napol

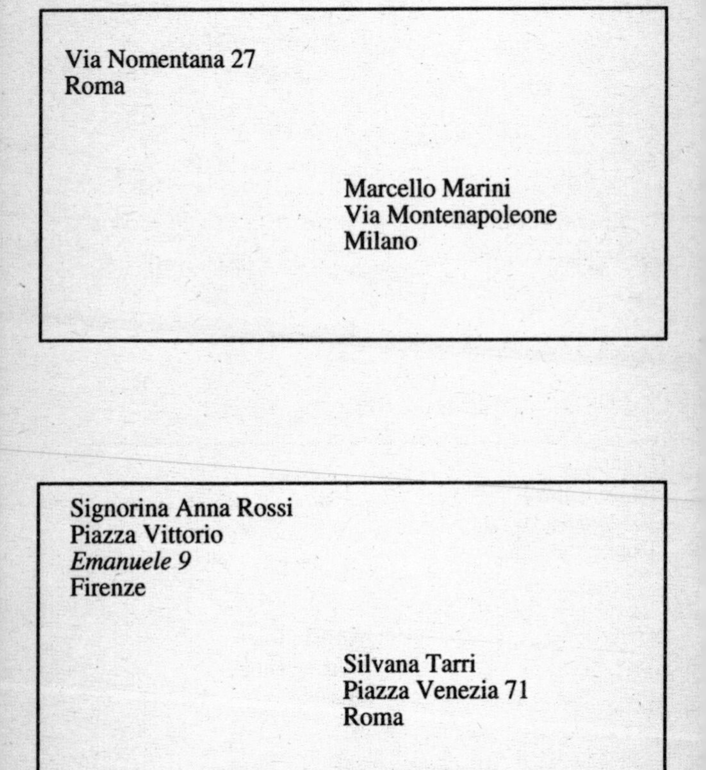
Via Nomentana 27
Roma
Marcello Marini
Via Montenapoleone
Milano
Signorina Anna Rossi
Piazza Vittorio
Emanuele 9
Firenze
Silvana Tarri
Piazza Venezia 71
Roma